# American Historical Fiction

## Second Edition

*by*

## A. T. Dickinson, Jr.

The Scarecrow Press, Inc.
New York          1963

L.C. Card No. 58-7803

"Fancy with fact is just one fact the more."

Robert Browning

## Preface

American historical fiction is a fascinating and informative field for study as evidenced by its popularity with the casual reader in library and bookstore, and its increasing use by teachers who recognize that fiction can bring to life for their students a particular period or event in history.

My own interest in the genre grew from the seed of an early interest in history, blossomed with the reading of "Gone With the Wind" and "The Red Badge of Courage," and bore first fruit in the form of a Master's thesis on the subject under the patient guidance of Professor Leon Carnovsky of the Graduate Library School, University of Chicago. This book is a direct descendant of that first effort.

Experience with the first edition revealed that its primary value was as a bibliography. I have, accordingly, tailored this second edition to that usage. The basic list consists of novels published from 1917 to 1961. I have, however, added those authors and titles which have come to be standard names in historical fiction regardless of publication date. No list of historical fiction, after all, is worthy of the name without "The Red Badge of Courage," or the works of James Fenimore Cooper, Winston Churchill, Mary Johnston, and others.

A total of 1,909 novels casting light on some aspect of American history are classified into periods of American history from Colonial days to the Cold War. The brief annotations are designed to place the books in historical perspective rather than to make any critical judgment.

5

A new category, "The Tense Years," has been added to cover novels dealing with the exciting years since the end of World War II. The Cold War, McCarthyism, the Korean War, the fight for racial equality, and occupation duty following World War II are major themes in fiction dealing with this period.

Another phase of American history which has come into being since World War II is our increasing involvement and interest in the social, political, economic, and ideological development of areas all over the world. At this point the line between historical fiction and contemporary fiction is thin indeed. If some selections in this area border on the international suspense and intrigue type of novel my defense is that they seemed to present a part of the picture of this involvement.

History moves inexorably and fiction follows close behind. It will be most interesting to watch fiction of the next few years for the appearance of the drama of orbital flight and space exploration as the background for novels of life in the nineteen-sixties.

Table of Contents

Introduction

Just what constitutes a historical novel is a question
which either plagues the person who would write about it, or
concerns him very little. At any rate, there are as many
definitions as there are definers. Perhaps the most suc-
cinct statement has been made by Ernest E. Leisy in "The
American Historical Novel:"

> In a sense all fiction has a preterit quality, a sense
> of having been lived. More specifically, historical
> fiction is concerned with historical truth, whatever
> that is. Whether such truth requires a spectacular
> historical figure or episode is a matter of controversy,
> as is the question of whether the term includes novels
> written contemporaneously with the events. Paul
> Leicester Ford once said "An historical novel is one
> which grafts upon a story actual incidents or persons
> well enough known to be recognized as historical
> elements." This definition appears too restrictive,
> however, for manners, customs, and ideas may suf-
> fice to identify a period... Owen Wister complicated
> the problem by asserting that "any narrative which
> presents a day and a generation is of necessity his-
> torical," a view concurred in by Brander Matthews
> when he said, "The really trustworthy historical novels
> are those which were a-writing while the history was
> a-making."

The statement of Owen Wister and Paul Leicester Ford
represent opposite extremes in the academic approach to
the definition of historical fiction. In practice, few would
disagree with Leisy that the historical novel is one in which
the action is laid in some identifiable past time. He suggests
that a generation seems sufficient to make a preceding period historical, and he ends his discussion with the period of

9

national expansion preceding World War I. His selection of
novels dealing with the Civil War, however, includes five
which were published during the years 1866 to 1873, one on
the Mexican War published in 1850, and one on the War of
1812 published in 1816. This would seem to bear out John
Hersey's contention that "the superior novel of contemporary
events will in time come to be regarded as a historical novel."

Robert A. Lively, in "Fiction Fights the Civil War,"
is not at all concerned with past time as a prerequisite for
the novels so ably analysed in his study of the Civil War in
fiction. His conclusion is that it is the "true residue of
fact or color which determines the value of a work as a
report from the past."

The criteria for judging whether a novel will, at a
given point in time, present to the reader a feeling for the
history potentially inherent in any piece of writing are: i-
dentifiable time, either by date or by approximate period;
identifiable place, either by definite locality or general
area; and an historical agent, whether a person, an event,
or a recognizable social, political, or economic phenomenon
characteristic of a period. Such a definition may be in-
terpreted with varying degrees of latitude, and offers the
reader interested in viewing our past through the novelist's
eyes wide scope in selection without concern about whether
the author was sufficiently removed from his subject to
rate the title of historical novelist.

American history, as rich and as varied as it is,
falls into a natural chronological pattern corresponding with
the periods of development of the nation from Colonial days
to the present, and this seems to be a logical arrange-
ment to follow. The usual breakdown of American history

includes the Colonial period, the period of the Revolution, a
period of national expansion on the frontier, Civil War and
Reconstruction, national development from the Civil War to
the turn of the century or to the first World War, World
War I, the period between the wars, and World War II.

With a few exceptions these periods adequately cover
the full scope of the novels of American history.  One exception is the growing body of  historical fiction dealing with
the political, social, and industrial development of the new
young nation in the years following the Revolution and ex-
tending into the first half of the 1800's which does not seem
to be properly classified with either the Revolution or with
the period of frontier expansion which followed.  These novels, including those dealing with the War of 1812, are
grouped under the heading "The Young Nation, 1783 to 1860."

A second exception is the group of novels dealing with
the period between World Wars I and II.  They are divided
into two groups, "The Twenties" and "The Thirties." Each
of these periods offers unique themes for the novelist to develop, as an examination of the novels will show.

A third exception is the period since World War II.
The years since the war have produced many crises which
have been reflected in fiction:  the Cold War, McCarthyism
and the loyalty investigations, the Korean War, the height-
ened interest in equality for the Negro, exemplified by the
forces leading up to the Supreme Court decision of 1954 and
the action of both factions since then, and our participation
in international diplomacy and the fight against Communism.
These are grouped under the heading, "The Tense Years."

"Chronicles" contains those novels which do not readily
fall into a single chronological period of history, but which,
nevertheless, are an important contribution to the fictional

literature of United States history--the epic novel which depicts a whole slice of American life, such as Sandburg's
"Remembrance Rock," or which follow a single family
through several generations, such as Hilda Morris' "The
Long View."

The historical novel is not limited to incidents or periods of crisis in a nation's history.  True, in each period,
from Colonial America to World War II and beyond, dramatic episodes have been used.  However, just as crises
are not the whole of a nation's history, so the novels of
crises are not the whole of historical fiction.  Conrad Richter, for instance, undeniably depicts an important element of
America's westward expansion in his series, and Irving Bacheller's "The Prodigal Village" is no less a historical novel of
the United States at the time of World War I than James
Wharton's "Squad."  Every phase of human endeavor and
interest--religion, politics, war, economics, and social and
cultural life--have been represented in fiction.

Colonial America to 1775

The colonial period has been the inspiration for novels dealing with a variety of themes. The period covered is that of the colonization and settlement of the original colonies, and of their political, economic, social, and religious development up to the time of the Revolution. The ill-fated settlement on Roanoke Island, the struggle for survival of the first settlement at Plymouth, Bacon's Rebellion, the Pontiac Conspiracy, the Yemassee Wars, the Deerfield raid, the Salem witchcraft trials, conflict between Quakers and Puritans, the New Hampshire land grant controversy, the attack on the French at Louisburg, Braddock's defeat, King Philip's War, and the siege of Fort Pitt are some of the more violent episodes in the history of the period which have been used in historical novels. Other novels have dealt with less violent, though not less crucial aspects of the period, such as the founding of Detroit, the French settlement of Mobile and New Orleans, social life at Williamsburg, the immigration of French Huguenots into the Carolinas and of the Scotch-Irish and Germans into Pennsylvania, the life of George Washington, and the social and mercantile life of the Dutch and the English in New York.

Alderman, Clifford Lindsey. Silver Keys. Putnam, 1960.
The adventures of William Phips in Boston, London, and the Caribbean before he became the first royal governor of Massachusetts under the charter of 1691.

Allen, Hervey. Bedford Village. Farrar, 1944. Picture

of Pennsylvania frontier life from 1763 to 1764. Sequel
to "Forest and the Fort."

\-- The Forest and the Fort. Farrar, 1943. The French
and Indian War in the forests of Pennsylvania in the
1760's, and the founding of Fort Pitt.

\-- Toward the Morning. Rinehart, 1948. Life on the
Pennsylvania frontier and in Philadelphia, 1764-1765.
Sequel to "Bedford Village" (above).

Allis, Marguerite. Not Without Peril. Putnam, 1941.
Pioneer hardships and folkways in the early settlement
of Vermont.

Aswell, Mary Louise. Abigail. Crowell, 1959. Background of colonial social and political life in Philadelphia in the story of a strong willed woman who rebelled against her Quaker environment.

Bacheller, Irving. Candle in the Wilderness. Bobbs, 1930.
Boston in stern colonial days; Reverend John Cotton,
Sir Harry Vane, and others appear.

Barker, Shirley. Peace, My Daughters. Crown, 1949.
Story of the witchcraft trials and persecutions in Salem in 1691.

\--- Rivers Parting, Crown, 1950. Settlement of New
Hampshire, and the struggle with Massachusetts over
control of the area.

\--- Swear by Apollo. Random, 1958. Picture of medical
and social life in New Hampshire in the years leading
up to the Revolution.

\--- Tomorrow the New Moon. Bobbs, 1955. Religious
conflict in Puritan New England in the days of Cotton

Mather in the early 1700's.

Barth, John. The Sot-Weed Factor. Doubleday, 1960. A
long, bawdy tale of many facets of life in colonial Maryland and England written in the style of the 17th century novelists.

Breslin, Howard. The Silver Oar. Crowell, 1954. Story
based on the revolt against Governor Andros in Boston
in 1689, with Cotton Mather as one of the characters.

Buchan, John. Salute to Adventurers. Doran, 1917. Adventure tale of colonial Virginia in 1690.

Cannon, LeGrand. Come Home at Even  Holt, 1951. Story
of four people who settle in the Puritan colony of Salem in the 1630's.

Coatsworth, Elizabeth. Sword of the Wilderness. Macmillan,
1936. Story of the French and Indian Wars in 1698 in
New England.

Colver, Alice. The Measure of the Years. Dodd, 1954.
Story of the white families who settled at Indian Town
(later Stockbridge) Massachusetts during the French
and Indian Wars. Pictures family life, religious controversy, Indian-white relations, and political events
leading up to the Revolution.

---  There is a Season. Dodd, 1957. Picture of family
life and frontier customs in Stockbridge, Massachusetts
and Charles-Town, South Carolina from 1756 to 1770.
Sequel to " Measure of the Years" (above).

Cooper, James Fenimore. The Deerslayer. Scribner, 1841.
Story of warfare between the Iroquois Indians and white
settlers around Lake Otsego, New York during King

George's War, 1744. Followed by "Last of the Mohicans."

--- The Last of the Mohicans. Scribner, 1826. Story of
wilderness warfare around Lake George, New York
during the French and Indian Wars. Followed by "The
Pathfinder."

--- The Pathfinder. Dodd, 1840. Tale of the French
and Indian War in the area around Lake Ontario. Followed by "The Pioneers."

--- The Pioneers. Dodd, 1822. Pioneer life in the wilderness around Lake Otsego, New York in the years
before the Revolution. Followed by "The Prairie"
(Expanding Frontiers - Middle West).

Cooper, Kent. Anna Zenger, Mother of Freedom. Farrar,
1946. Story of the first newspaper in New York and
the first battle for freedom of the press, set against
a background of life under the British governors.

Coryell, Hubert. Indian Brother. Harcourt, 1935. Adventures of a young colonist and his sister captured by
the Indians; Maine in 1713.

--- Scalp Hunters. Harcourt, 1936. Experiences of a
young colonist and his Indian brother in Maine in the
early 1700's.

Costain, Thomas B. High Towers. Doubleday, 1949. Adventures of the LeMoyne brothers who explored the
Mississippi River and founded New Orleans and Mobile
in the early 1700's.

Cross, Ruth. Soldier of Good Fortune. Banks Upshaw,
1936. Exploits of Louis de St. Denis on a trading ex-

pedition into Texas and Mexico for the French colony
at Mobile in 1715.

Curwood, James Oliver.  The Plains of Abraham.  Doubleday, 1928.  Romance of the French-English wars leading up to the capture of Quebec.

Devon, John Anthony.  O Western Wind.  Putnam, 1957.
Story of the founding of Merry Mount and of its destruction by Miles Standish; emphasis on the bigotry and intolerance of the Puritans of the Pilgrim colony at Plymouth.

Dodge, Constance.  In Adam's Fall.  Macrae, 1946.  Story
of the Salem witchcraft hysteria of the seventeenth century; recreates the life and spirit of the times.

Dowdey, Clifford.  Gamble's Hundred.  Little, 1939.  Tidewater Virginia around 1730; scene is mostly in Williamsburg.

Eaton, Evelyn.  Restless Are the Sails.  Harper, 1941.  Historical romance centering around the fall of Louisburg
in 1745.

---  The Sea Is So Wide.  Harper, 1943.  Story of French
Acadians banished from their farmland in Nova Scotia
during the French-English war who settle in the Southern colonies; pictures social life in Williamsburg.

Etheridge, Willie Snow.  Summer Thunder.  Coward, 1959.
Founding of Savannah and the early colonization of
Georgia in the 1730's; picture of James Oglethorpe.

Fletcher, Inglis.  Bennett's Welcome.  Bobbs, 1950. Story
of the first permanent settlement of North Carolina,
still part of Virginia in 1651-1652.  See other novels

in this series under "The American Revolution" and
"The Young Nation."

--- Cormorant's Brood. Lippincott, 1959. Pictures the
struggle of the colonists in the Albemarle region of
North Carolina against their weak but greedy royal
governors;1725-1729.

--- Lusty Wind for Carolina. Bobbs, 1944. Story of the
North Carolina plantation owners and of their attempts
to establish communities and ward off pirates destroy-
ing their trade; 1718-1725.

--- Men of Albemarle. Bobbs, 1942. The evolution of
law and order in colonial North Carolina; 1710-1712.

--- Roanoke Hundred. Bobbs, 1948. Story of the first
British settlement in America; scenes laid in England
of Elizabethan times and in the wilderness of Roanoke
Island; 1585-1586; Sir Richard Grenville, Sir Walter
Raleigh, and others appear.

--- The Wind in the Forest. Bobbs, 1957. Story of the
Regulator's Insurrection in North Carolina, an uprising
of frontier farmers against the royal governor, William
Tyron, and the Tidewater planters; ends in the Battle
of Alamance in 1771.

Forbes, Esther. A Morror For Witches. Houghton, 1928.
Amusing picture of a Massachusetts village during the
witchcraft hysteria.

--- Paradise. Harcourt, 1937. Settlement of Canaan,
near Boston, in the Massachusetts Bay Colony at the
time of King Philip's War.

Frey, Ruby Frazier. Red Morning. Putnam, 1946. Back-

ground of the struggle for the Ohio valley; warfare
between Indians, French, and English in which George
Washington began his career; Governor Dinwiddie,
Franklin, and Braddock appear.

Fuller, Iola. The Gilded Torch. Putnam, 1957. Story of
the explorations of LaSalle in the Great Lakes and
Mississippi River areas and of his attempt to set up
a French empire in America in the 1680's and 1690's.

Gebler, Ernest. Plymouth Adventure. Doubleday, 1950.
Story of the Mayflower Pilgrims from Southampton
across the Atlantic through the first few months on
the New England coast.

Gerson, Noel B. Daughter of Eve. Doubleday, 1958.
Story of Captain John Smith and Pocahontas; picture of
the life and customs of the Indians and the English in
the early days of the Virginia colony at Jamestown.

--- The Highwayman. Doubleday, 1955. Story built a-
round the expedition against the French at Louisburg
during the French and Indian War, 1744-1748.

Giles, Janice Holt. Hannah Fowler. Houghton, 1956. Story
of pioneer settlers on the Kentucky River in the 1770's.

Gordon, Caroline. The Green Centuries. Scribner, 1941.
Pre-Revolutionary life in pioneer Kentucky and Tennessee; picture of the settlement of the Holston River
area, and of the negotiations between the Indians and
Judge Henderson.

Hawthorne, Nathaniel. The Scarlet Letter. Dodd, 1850.
Tale of sin and retribution in Puritan Boston.

Hughes, Rupert. Stately Timber. Scribner, 1939. Life in

Puritan New England and in Virginia and the Barbados
Islands in the 1650's.

Jennings, John. Gentleman Ranker. Reynal, 1942. Story
of an English dandy tricked into joining Braddock's
expedition against the French in 1755; settles in A-
merica and adapts himself to frontier life.

--- Next to Valour. Macmillan, 1939. Roger's Rangers
in New Hampshire during the French and Indian
Wars; 1750's.

Johnston, Mary. Croatan. Little, 1923. Story of the ill-
fated Roanoke settlement in Virginia in 1587. Heroine
is Virginia Dare.

--- Great Valley. Little, 1926. Virginia before and during the French and Indian Wars; 1737-1759.

--- Prisoners of Hope. Houghton, 1898. Colonial life in
Virginia centering around the deportation of convicts to
the colony from England; 1649-1651.

--- The Slave Ship. Little, 1924. Story of the colonial
slave trade; 1660's.

--- To Have and To Hold. Houghton, 1900. Story set in
Virginia in 1621 centering around the first shipload of
brides sent to the colony.

Jordan, Mildred. One Red Rose Forever. Knopf, 1941.
Pennsylvania of the mid-1700's; hero is Baron Stiegel,
the German immigrant who became known as the maker
of Stiegel glass.

King, Grace. La Dame de Sainte Hermine. Macmillan,
1924. Story of the settlement of New Orleans by Pierre
LeMoyne in 1718.

Lide, Alice. Dark Possession. Appleton, 1934. Charles
    Town, South Carolina in the early 1700's; a tale of
    slaves and indentured servants, Indian wars, sorcery,
    and passion.

Lincoln, Victoria. A Dangerous Innocence. Rinehart, 1958.
    Life in Salem, Massachusetts at the time of the witch-
    craft trials.

Lofts, Norah. Blossom Like the Rose. Knopf, 1939. Ro-
    mance of a young Scotsman who joins a band of reli-
    gious fanatics, sails to America, and battles Indians
    and Puritan intolerance.

Lovelace, Maud Hart. Charming Sally. Day, 1932. Story
    of the first theatrical company to come to America;
    picture of brilliant social life in Virginia and more se-
    date Quaker life in Philadelphia in 1752.

Malvern, Gladys. Eric's Girls. Messner, 1949. New
    Amsterdam, the Dutch city of Peter Stuyvesant at the
    time of the English siege and capture.

Mann, Helen. Gallant Warrior. William B. Eerdmans,
    1954. Fictionized biography of Hannah Duston, pioneer
    wife and mother who, with her baby and its nurse, was
    captured by Indians in 1697; recreates the spirit of the
    period.

Marsh, George. Ask No Quarter. Morrow, 1945. Newport,
    Rhode Island at the end of the 17th century; recon-
    structs the speech and details of daily life of the period.

Mason, Van Wyck. The Young Titan. Doubleday, 1959.
    Story of the hazards of frontier living during the French
    and Indian War; scenes set in Boston, in Bartholomey

Mayhew's settlement on the Penobscot River, and on
the wilderness march against Louisburg in 1745.

Matschat, Cecile Hulse. Tavern in the Town. Farrar,
1942. A romance of plantation life in colonial Virginia.

Miers, Earl Schenck. Valley in Arms. Westminster, 1943.
Clearing the land and fighting Indians in a Connecticut
valley in the 1630's.

Miller, Helen Topping. Dark Sails. Bobbs, 1945. Oglethorpe's colonization of Georgia in the 1730's and 1740's.

Moore, Ruth. A Fair Wind Home. Morrow, 1953. Story
of Nathan Ellis of Massachusetts, Francis Carnavon of
Cork, and Maynard Cantril, a shipbuilder of Somerset,
Maine before the Revolution.

Murphy, Edward. A Bride for New Orleans. Hanover,
1955. Historical romance of the Casket girls sent to
New Orleans from Paris in 1727 to marry and to help
settle Louisiana.

Newton, John Edward. The Rogue and the Witch. Abelard,
1955. Story of religious conflict between Puritans and
Quakers in Boston, involving the Salem witchcraft
trials; Increase Mather is one of the characters.

Oemler, Marie. The Holy Lover. Boni and Liveright, 1927.
Story of John Wesley, dealing with the three years he
spent in the Georgia colony, 1735-1738; based on jour-
nals and letters from the period.

Page, Elizabeth. Wilderness Adventure. Rinehart, 1946.
A tale of the rescue of a young girl captured by Indians; rescuers follow her from Virginia to the Mississippi River, to New Orleans, and on to France and

England

Paradise, Jean.  The Savage City.  Crown, 1955.  Story of
    colonial New York, based on the hysteria caused by a
    servant girl's tale of a Negro-Spanish plot to massacre
    the whites in the city.

Parker, Sir Gilbert.  The Power and the Glory.  Harper,
    1925.  Achievements of LaSalle as pioneer and ex-
    plorer; a novel of early Canadian and American history.

Pendexter, Hugh.  The Red Road.  Bobbs, 1927.  Tale of
    Braddock's defeat during the French and Indian War,
    1754-1763.

---  Wife-Ship Woman.  Louisiana and Virginia in the early
    1700's; heroine is one of the Casket girls sent from
    France to be the wives of men in the Louisiana colony
    at New Orleans in 1727.

Phillips, Alexandra.  Forever Possess.  Dutton, 1946.  Pic-
    ture of life on the feudal estates on the Hudson River
    in New York in the 17th century at the time of an up-
    rising among the tenants.

Pinckney, Josephine.  Hilton Head, Farrar, 1941.  Story of
    the tribulations of a young doctor in South Carolina in
    the 1600's.

Pound, Arthur.  The Hawk of Detroit.  Reynal, 1939. The
    founding of Detroit, and conflicting interests in the
    government monopoly of trade; Chief Cadillac is one
    of the characters.

Rees, Gilbert.  I Seek a City.  Dutton, 1950.  Fictional
    autobiography of Roger Williams, from his early life
    in England, his voyage to the colonies, his work as

a minister in Salem, Massachusetts, his founding of
Providence, Rhode Island, and his understanding of the
Indians.

Richter, Conrad. Free Man. Knopf, 1943. Story of a
young emigrant from the Palatinate who sought political freedom among the Pennsylvania-Dutch.

--- The Light in the Forest. Knopf, 1953. Settlers and
Indians in Pennsylvania and Ohio at the time of Bou-
quet's expedition to free the captives of the Tuscarawas
Indians in 1765.

Ritchie, Cicero T. The Willing Maid. Abelard, 1958. Boston and Nova Scotia during the French and Indian War;
climax comes at the fall of Louisburg; 1740's.

Roberts, Kenneth L. Boon Island. Doubleday, 1956. Story
of the harrowing experience of the survivors of a ship-
wreck on an island near Portsmouth, New Hampshire
in 1710.

--- Northwest Passage. Doubleday, 1937. Major Robert
Rogers, and his expedition against the Indians of St.
Francis in 1759. His dream was to find an overland
passage to the Pacific.

Safford, Henry B. Tristram Bent. Coward, 1940. Hero
is an English agent sent to spy on the Dutch colonies
in 1640; accurate historical details of the period and
place.

Sass, Herbert R. Emperor Brims. Doubleday, 1941. The
Yemassee War in South Carolina in 1715; uprising of
the Creek Indian Confederacy against the white settlements on the coast.

Schachner, Nathan. The King's Passenger. Lippincott,
    1942. Colonial Virginia at the time of Bacon's Rebel-
    lion and the burning of Jamestown in 1676.

Seifert, Shirley. River Out of Eden. M.S. Mill, 1940.
    Trip up the Mississippi River from New Orleans to
    the settlement later known as St. Louis in 1763; pic-
    tures political and economic rivalries on the frontier.

Seton, Anya. The Winthrop Woman. Houghton, 1958. Story
    of the Massachusetts Bay Colony and Connecticut,
    based on the life of Governor John Winthrop's niece;
    an account of life in early Boston.

Settle, Mary Lee. O Beulah Land. Viking, 1956. Pic-
    tures the hardships of a group of Virginia settlers in
    the wilderness beyond the Allegheny Mountains and
    their struggles with the French and Indians; 1754-1774.

Simms, William Gilmore. The Yemassee. 1835. Colonial
    expansion seen from the viewpoint of the Indians; story
    of the events leading up to the Yemassee War in South
    Carolina in the early 1700's.

Simons, Katherine. Always a River. Appleton, 1956. Story
    of the clash of temperaments between a Puritan school-
    master, who leaves Massachusetts during the witch-
    craft hysteria, and the French Huguenots in the Car-
    olinas in 1695.

---    The Land Beyond the Tempest. Coward, 1960. Story
    of a hazardous voyage from England to colonial James-
    town, Virginia.

Singmaster, Elsie. A High Wind Rising. Houghton, 1942.
    Story of life in a Pennsylvania German-Dutch settle-

ment at the time of the French and Indian War; based
on the life of Conrad Weiser and his relations with the
Indians.

Smith, Arthur Douglas. The Doom Trail. Brentano, 1922.
Story built on the struggle for supremacy in the fur
trade between the French and the English.

Snedeker, Caroline. Uncharted Ways. Doubleday, 1935.
Based on the life of Mary Dyer, a Quaker convert in
Boston in the 1650's; pictures the religious tension of
the period, and John Cotton's persecution of the Quakers.

Stanford, Alfred B. The Navigator. Morrow, 1927. Biography of Nathaniel Bowditch, creator of "The American Practical Navigator" in Salem in the 1770's.

Stone, Grace Zaring. The Cold Journey. Morrow, 1934.
Story of the 1704 raid on Deerfield, Massachusetts by
French and Indians and the long hard journey of the
captives to Quebec; contrasts life and manners of the
French and the Puritans.

Stover, Herbert. Song of the Susquehanna. Dodd, 1949.
Story of a Pennsylvania-German's battle with Indians
during the French and Indian War; Governeur Morris,
John Bartram, and Conrad Weiser appear in the story.

Stowman, Knud. With Cradle and Clock. Harper, 1946.
Struggles of a young doctor to establish an obstetrical
practice in New York in 1702; background of New York
social life and customs.

Sublette, Clifford. The Bright Face of Danger. Little, 1926.
Life in Henrico County, Virginia in the days of Bacon's

Rebellion; 1676.

--- Scarlet Cockerel. Little, 1925. Historical romance
based on the French Huguenot colonization of the Carolinas in the 1690's.

Swanson, Neil. The First Rebel. Farrar, 1937. Story of
the uprising of the Scotch-Irish in Pennsylvania, led by
James Smith, against the British and of Smith's capture
by the Indians; 1763-1767.

--- The Judas Tree. Putnam, 1933. Pittsburg besieged
by the Indians during the Pontiac Conspiracy of 1763.

--- The Silent Drum. Farrar, 1940. Life on the Pennsylvania frontier during the pre-Revolutionary period.

--- The Unconquered. Doubleday, 1947. Story of the
Pontiac Conspiracy of 1763 in the Ohio River region of
the Pennsylvania frontier.

Van Every, Dale. Bridal Journey. Messner, 1950. Story
of life in the Ohio River valley when Indians, English,
and Americans were fighting for the frontier lands
prior to the Revolution.

Vaughan, Carter. The Invincibles. Doubleday, 1958. Financial scheming and frontier warfare during the
French and Indian Wars, set in and around Boston and
in the wilderness on the expedition against Louisburg;
1744-1745.

Widdemer, Margaret. Buckskin Baronet. Doubleday, 1960.
Story of an English traveler in and around Albany,
New York on the eve of the Revolution; picture of In-
dian customs and the political intrigues of the time.

--- The Golden Wildcat. Doubleday, 1954. Historical

romance depicting the struggle between British and French for the loyalty of the Mohawks and Iroquois Indians in upstate New York in the 1750's.

--- Lady of the Mohawks. Doubleday, 1951. Story of French and English rivalry in the Mohawk Valley; the heroine is Molly Brant, who became the wife of Sir William Johnson, English Indian Commissioner.

Winwar, Frances. Gallows Hill. Holt, 1937. Story of early times in old Salem, chiefly concerned with the religious frenzy which took possession of the colony leading to the witchcraft trials and hangings; Cotton Mather appears.

Zara, Louis. Blessed is the Land. Crown, 1954. Set in the days of Peter Stuyvesant when the first Jewish settlers came from Brazil to settle in New Amsterdam; picture of Jewish customs, language, and religion in the colonial period.

The American Revolution

The American Revolution has been well documented in
historical fiction, from the tense political situation leading
to the Battles of Lexington and Concord, through the progress of the war southward to its culmination in Cornwallis'
surrender at Yorktown, the war on the frontier, and the development of the American navy under Commodore John Paul
Jones. The Boston Tea Party, the terrible winter at Valley
Forge, Benjamin Franklin's diplomatic mission to France,
the career of Benedict Arnold, the activities of George Rogers Clark on the frontier and of Francis Marion in South
Carolina, the neutrality of Westchester County, New York
and the conflict between English and rebel loyalties through-
out the colonies, the separatist movement on the frontiers of
Kentucky and Tennessee and the founding of the Transylvania
Company and the state of Franklin, as well as action leading
to various battles and campaigns of the war are some of the
subjects of novels dealing with this period of history.

Allen, Merritt Parmalee. Battle Lanterns. Longmans, 1949.
    Exploits of Francis Marion, the Swamp Fox, and the
    war in South Carolina.

Bacheller, Irving. In the Days of Poor Richard. Bobbs,
    1922. Shows the work of Franklin in the colonies, in
    England, and in France; comprehensive picture of the
    Revolution.

--- Master of Chaos. Bobbs, 1932. Early days of the
    Revolution; George Washington and others appear.

Barker, Shirley.  Fire and the Hammer.  Crown, 1953.
    Story of Quaker outlaws in Bucks County, Pennsylvania
    harrassing the Revolutionists.

---  The Last Gentleman.  Random, 1960.  Story of the
    conflicts facing the colonial born Sir John Wentworth,
    royal governor of New Hampshire in 1774; climax
    comes when he sends aid to General Gage in Boston in
    1775.

Barry, Jane.  The Carolinians.  Doubleday, 1959.  A Loy-
    alist family in South Carolina becomes involved in the
    war when they help one of General Dan Morgan's men;
    action includes the Battles of Cowpens and King's
    Mountain.

---  The Long March.  Appleton, 1955.  Portrait of Gen-
    eral Dan Morgan in the campaign culminating the Bat-
    tle of Cowpens.

Beebe, Elswyth Thane.  Dawn's Early Light.  Duell, 1943.
    The Carolina campaigns of the war, and politics and
    society in Williamsburg; 1774-1779.

Benét, Stephen Vincent.  Spanish Bayonet.  Doran, 1926.
    Adventure tale set in New York and Spanish Florida at
    the time of the Revolution.

Beverley-Giddings, Arthur Raymond.  The Rival Shores.
    Morrow, 1956.  Story of an Englishman sent to the
    colonies to aid the escape of Loyalists from Tidewater
    Maryland in 1774.

Boyce, Burke.  Man From Mt. Vernon.  Harper, 1961.
    Personal and family life of George Washington from
    his appointment as Commander-in-Chief of the Con-
    tinental army to the surrender of the British at York-

town.

--- The Perilous Night. Viking, 1942. The war as it
affected the prosperous Hudson River valley farmers,
with firm convictions of loyalty either to the king or
to the colonies.

Boyd, James. Drums. Scribner, 1925. The war in the
southern colonies; John Paul Jones, Generals Dan
Morgan, and Tarleton appear.

Boyd, Thomas Alexander. Shadow of the Long Knives.
Scribner, 1928. Story of the Ohio frontier during the
Revolution.

Brick, John. The King's Rangers. Doubleday, 1954. Story
of Butler's Rangers and Loyalists in the western Mohawk Valley area of New York.

--- The Raid. Farrar, 1951. The Mohawk chief, Joseph
Brant, leading his tribe in raids against the settlers in
upstate New York.

--- The Rifleman. Doubleday, 1953. Story of Tim Murphy,
one of Morgan's riflemen, and of his grudge against the
Indians; description of the Battle of Saratoga.

--- Strong Men. Doubleday, 1959. Story of a company of
rangers with Washington at Valley Forge in the winter of
1777-1778, and of Baron von Steuben's efforts to mold
the survivors into an effective army.

Bristow, Gwen. Celia Garth. Crowell, 1959. Story of an
orphan girl who witnessed the siege of Charleston by
the British, and became a spy for the rebels during the
occupation of the city; description of the fighting between
General Tarleton and Francis Marion's raiders.

Cannon, LeGrand. Look to the Mountain. Holt, 1942.
Frontier days in New Hampshire just before and after
the Revolution.

Chambers, Robert W. Little Red Foot. Doran, 1921. Indian warfare in northeastern New York, 1774-1782.

--- The Painted Minx. Appleton, 1930. Life in New York
City during the years 1777-1781.

Chapman, Maristan (pseud.). Rogue's March. Lippincott,
1949. Skirmishing in western Carolina and Tennessee
culminating in the Battle of King's Mountain in 1780.

Churchill, Winston. The Crossing. Macmillan, 1904. Life
on the Kentucky frontier during the Revolution; George
Rogers Clark's expedition against Vincennes and Kas-
kaskia; life in early Louisville; and a picture of New
Orleans during an epidemic.

--- Richard Carvel. Macmillan, 1899. Set in Maryland
and London before and during the Revolution; hero
fights with John Paul Jones in the battle between the
"Bon Homme Richard" and the "Serapis."

Coatsworth, Elizabeth. A Toast to the King. Coward, 1940.
Boston at the time of the Boston Tea Party, seen from
the Loyalists' viewpoint.

Cooper, James Fenimore. The Pilot. Dodd, 1824. Story
of John Paul Jones and naval warfare during the Revolution.

--- The Red Rover. Putnam, 1827. An adventure story
of a former pirate fighting for his country during the
Revolution.

--- The Spy. Dodd, 1821. Story of conflicting loyalties in
New York City and the Hudson valley.

Cormack, Maribelle, and William P. Alexander. Land For
My Sons. Appleton, 1939. A surveyor and wilderness
scout on the Pennsylvania frontier sees action as a
member of the local militia when war breaks out.

Davis, Burke. The Ragged Ones. Rinehart, 1951. Southern
campaign of 1781 with Generals Morgan and Nathanael
Greene engaging the forces under Cornwallis.

--- Yorktown. Rinehart, 1952. Portrait of Washington,
Lafayette, Clinton, and Cornwallis in the campaign
leading up to Cornwallis' surrender at Yorktown.

Davis, William Stearns. Gilman of Redford. Macmillan,
1927. Story of Boston and Harvard College on the
eve of the Revolution, 1770-1775; pictures life and
customs in town and country, and revolves around
famous men and events of the period; Paul Revere,
Samuel Adams, and others appear.

Decker, Malcolm. The Rebel and the Turncoat. McGraw,
1949. A young colonist torn between loyalty to the
British and the American cause chooses sides with the
help of Nathan Hale.

Dodge, Constance. Dark Stranger. Penn, 1940. Son of
Scotch settlers fights under John Paul Jones on the
"Bon Homme Richard."

Eaton, Evelyn. Give Me Your Golden Hand. Farrar, 1951.
Eighteenth century England and America; events leading up to the Revolution are seen through the eyes of
the hero who comes to the colonies as a bonded servant
during the Revolution.

Edmonds, Walter D. Drums Along the Mohawk. Little,
1936. Affects of the Revolution on the farmers of the

Mohawk Valley in upstate New York, 1776-1784.

--- In the Hands of the Senecas. Little, 1947. Indian
warfare on the frontier in 1778; story of the captivity
of a group of children held by the Senecas.

--- Wilderness Clearing. Dodd, 1944. Story of conflict
and divided loyalties in the Mohawk Valley in 1777.

Ellsberg, Edward. Captain Paul. Dodd, 1941. John Paul
Jones from his days as a privateer to the engagement
with the "Serapis."

Erskine, John. Give Me Liberty. Stokes, 1940. Patrick
Henry, George Washington, and Thomas Jefferson appear in a story of a young Virginian from 1759 to the
outbreak of the Revolution.

Fast, Howard. April Morning. Crown, 1961. Experiences
of a 15 year old farm boy in the Battles of Lexington
and Concord; April, 1775.

--- Citizen Tom Paine. Duell, 1943. Portrait of Tom
Paine as a rabble-rouser.

--- Conceived in Liberty. Simon and Schuster, 1939.
Alexander Hamilton, von Stueben, Valley Forge; picture of the contrast between the ragged soldiers and
the wealthy aristocrats in the Continental army.

--- The Proud and the Free. Little, 1950. Based on a
revolt in the Continental army against injustices by the
officers of the Pennsylvania militia.

--- The Unvanquished. Duell, 1942. Portrays Washington,
Knox, Putnam, Greene, and Hamilton and their part
in the fight for freedom from the retreat from Brooklyn
to the crossing of the Delaware and the Battle of

Trenton.

Fletcher, Inglis.  Raleigh's Eden.  Bobbs, 1940.  Life in
North Carolina from 1765 to 1782; one of the author's
series on the history of North Carolina ("Colonial A-
merica" and "The Young Nation").

--- The Scotswoman.  Bobbs, 1954.  Flora McDonald, who
rescued Bonnie Prince Charlie after the Battle of Cul-
leden, settles in the Carolinas and becomes involved
in the American Revolution.

--- Toil of the Brave.  Bobbs, 1946.  The Albemarle
district of North Carolina in the last years of the war,
1779-1780.

Forbes, Esther.  The General's Lady.  Harcourt, 1938.
Girl of a New England Tory family marries a rebel
general to save her family's fortune, then falls in love
with a British officer.

--- Johnny Tremain.  Houghton, 1943.  Boston at the beginning of the Revolution; the Boston Tea Party, the
Battle of Lexington; young hero is a courier for the
rebel Committee of Public Safety.

Ford, Paul Leicester.  Janice Meredith.  Dodd, 1899.  Beginning in New Jersey in 1774, this spans the years of
the Revolution and includes a picture of the character
of George Washington.

Fox, John.  Erskine Dale, Pioneer.  Scribner, 1920.  Life
on the Virginia and Kentucky frontier at the time of
the Revolution.

Frye, Pearl.  Gallant Captain.  Little, 1956.  Story of John
Paul Jones, from his days as an obscure British ship

commander to the hero of the American navy; authentic picture of the times.

Gessner, Robert. Treason. Scribner, 1944. Fictional biography of Benedict Arnold.

Giles, Janice Holt. The Kentuckians. Houghton, 1953. Story of pioneer Kentucky when the Transylvania Company was agitating for separate statehood; 1769-1777.

Gordon, Charles William. The Rebel Loyalist. Dodd, 1935. Story of a Loyalist who fought on the side of the British in the war, and afterward took his bride to Canada.

Graves, Robert. Proceed, Sergeant Lamb. Random, 1941. English soldier's experiences as a prisoner, his escape, service under Cornwallis, and the surrender at Yorktown. Sequel to "Sergeant Lamb's America."

--- Sergeant Lamb's America. Random, 1940. Experiences of an English soldier in the early years of the war.

Gray, Elizabeth Janet. Meggy MacIntosh. Doubleday, 1930. Story of a young Scotch girl who joins Flora Mac Donald in North Carolina in 1775.

--- The Virginia Exiles. Lippincott, 1955. Story of the exile of a group of Philadelphia Quakers to Virginia when they refuse to sign a loyalty oath.

Grey, Zane. Betty Zane. Grosset, 1903. Tale of hardships of life beyond the Allegheny Mountains on the Virginia frontier; fights with the Indians and the destruction of the settlement during the Revolution.

Haines, Edwin. The Exquisite Siren. Lippincott, 1938. Historical novel about Peggy Shippen, Tory wife of Benedict Arnold, and her relations with Major André.

Haislip, Harvey. The Prize Master. Doubleday, 1959.
Story of sea warfare during the Revolution through the
adventures of a young seaman introduced in "Sailor
Named Jones" (below).

--- Sailor Named Jones. Doubleday, 1957. Story of John
Paul Jones and of his financial difficulties and lack of
support from the government; vivid recreation of naval
warfare, culminating in the battle of the "Bon Homme
Richard" and the "Serapis."

--- Sea Road to Yorktown. Doubleday, 1960. Further adventures of the hero of "The Prize Master" (above) as
a privateer and on duty with the fleet of Admiral de
Grasse in Chesapeake Bay blocking Cornwallis' escape
from Yorktown.

Harris, Cyril. Richard Pryne. Scribner, 1941. Story of
a spy for General Washington in and around New York
City.

--- Trumpet at Dawn. Scribner, 1938. New York social
life and politics, 1776-1783.

Henri, Florette. Kings Mountain. Doubleday, 1950. Story
of the war in the southern colonies; Battle of King's
Mountain, South Carolina in 1780.

Horan, James David. The King's Rebel. Crown, 1953.
Story of a British officer sent to study the Indians;
captured by the backwoodsmen, he comes to know them
and joins their cause.

Horne, Howard. Concord Bridge. Bobbs, 1952. Story of
the events preceding the Battles of Lexington and Concord; sympathetic portrait of General Gage, commander

of the English forces at Boston.

Hough, Frank Olney. If Not Victory. Lippincott, 1939. The
war from the viewpoint of the common man; setting is
the Hudson River valley of New York.

---  The Neutral Ground. Lippincott, 1941. The affects of
the war on the neutral Westchester County region of
New York.

---  Renown. Lippincott, 1938. Sympathetic account of
Benedict Arnold, showing him as a brilliant, extra-
vagant, and frustrated man of action.

Jennings, John. The Sea Eagles. Doubleday, 1950. Story
of the young American navy and its part in the war.

---  The Shadow and the Glory. Reynal, 1943. Centers
around the campaigns leading up to the Battle of Bennington, 1774-1777.

Johnston, Mary. Hunting Shirt. Little, 1931. Life in a
Cherokee Indian village in the Virginia wilderness,
1775-1780.

Karig, Walter and Horace Bird. Don't Tread On Me. Rinehart, 1954. Exploits of Commodore John Paul Jones;
picture of early American politics, naval warfare, and
social life.

Kelly, Eric. Three Sides of Agiochook. Macmillan, 1935.
Life on the New England frontier in 1775.

Lancaster, Bruce. The Blind Journey. Little, 1953. Benjamin Franklin sends money and supplies from France
by a courier who lands near Yorktown in time for the
campaign against Cornwallis.

--- Guns of Burgoyne. Stokes, 1939. Story of the defeat
of Burgoyne at the Battle of Saratoga from the viewpoint of a Hessian officer.

--- The Phantom Fortress. Little, 1950. Story of the
guerrilla warfare of Francis Marion, the Swamp Fox,
in the Carolinas.

--- The Secret Road. Little, 1952. Story of the part
Washington's secret service played in exposing Bene-
dict Arnold's treason and in the capture of Major
André; picture of wartime life in New York City under
British occupation.

--- Trumpet to Arms. Little, 1944. Story of local militia companies in the campaigns of the war up to the
Battle of Trenton.

Leland, John Adams. Othneil Jones. Lippincott, 1956.
The war in the Carolinas as seen by a member of
Francis Marion's raiders.

Linington, Elizabeth. The Long Watch. Viking, 1956.
Story of two colonial newspaper editors and of their
struggle to keep their newspapers operating during the
war; picture of life in New York City in the 1770's
before the war and during the British occupation.

Lynde, Francis. Mr. Arnold. Bobbs, 1923. Story of
Benedict Arnold centering around an attempt to kidnap
Arnold and bring him back for trial after his escape.

Mason, Van Wyck. Eagle in the Sky. Lippincott, 1948.
The role of the navy in the final campaign at Yorktown; 1780-1781.

--- Rivers of Glory. Lippincott, 1942. Story centering

around the seige of the British forces in Savannah;
1778-1779.

---   Stars On the Sea. Lippincott, 1940. Picture of the
war in Rhode Island, Charleston, and the Bahamas;
1776-1777.

---   Three Harbors. Lippincott, 1938. First in the author's series on the role of the American navy in the
war; setting is Norfolk and Boston; 1774-1775.

Melville, Herman. Israel Potter. Putnam, 1855. Based on
the life of a Revolutionary war hero who fought at
Bunker Hill, served as messenger to Benjamin Franklin, and served under John Paul Jones in the battle of
the "Bon Homme Richard" and the "Serapis."

Mercer, Charles. Enough Good Men. Putnam, 1960. Picture of the political background of the war, and of
social life in Philadelphia.

Miller, Helen Topping. Christmas at Mount Vernon. Longmans, 1957. Short novel picturing the homecoming
and Christmas celebration of George and Martha Washington at Mount Vernon in December, 1783.

---   Slow Dies the Thunder. Bobbs, 1955. Romance set
against a background of the war in South Carolina in
1780; the bombardment of Charleston, Francis Marion's
guerrilla warfare, and the Battle of King's Mountain.

---   The Sound of Chariots. Bobbs, 1947. A Loyalist
family flees from Augusta, Georgia to John Sevier's
state of Franklin on the frontier after the Battle of
King's Mountain.

Minnegerode, Meade. The Black Forest. Farrar, 1937.

Story of life in the Northwest Territory from 1754
through the Revolution.

Mitchell, S. Weir. Hugh Wynne, Free Quaker. Century,
1897. Life in Philadelphia during the war; hero serves
as a spy for Washington and Lafayette.

Nutt, Frances. Three Fields to Cross. Stephen-Paul,
1947. Spy story set in Staten Island, New York.

Page, Elizabeth. Tree of Liberty. Farrar, 1939. A panorama of national events from 1754 to 1806.

Patterson, Emma. Midnight Patriot. Longmans, 1949.
Heroic activities of a young colonist in the early days
of the Revolution.

Pridgen, Tim. Tory Oath. Doubleday, 1941. Highland
Scots of the Carolinas take the king's side in the Revolution.

Raddall, Thomas. His Majesty's Yankees. Winston, 1943.
New Englanders living in Nova Scotia at the outbreak
of the Revolution are torn between allegiance to the
Crown and to the cause of the colonies.

Ripley, Clements. Clear for Action. Appleton, 1940. John
Paul Jones and the "Bon Homme Richard."

Roberts, Kenneth L. Arundel. Doubleday, 1930. Setting is
Arundel, Maine. Describes Benedict Arnold's expedition against Quebec.

--- Oliver Wiswell. Doubleday, 1940. Presents the Loyalists' side of the war.

--- Rabble in Arms. Doubleday, 1933. Story of the
campaign leading up to the Battle of Saratoga; hero is

Benedict Arnold; villian is Continental Congress.

Sabatini, Rafael. The Carolinian. Houghton, 1925. Historical romance set in South Carolina during the war.

Safford, Henry B. That Bennington Mob. Messner, 1935.
Story of the settlers in the New Hampshire grants,
their relations with the Indians, and the actions leading to the Battle of Bennington in 1777.

Schoonover, Lawrence. The Revolutionary. Little, 1958.
Biographical novel of John Paul Jones, from boyhood
in Scotland, through the American Revolution, service
in Russia under Catherine the Great, to his death in
Paris in 1792.

Seifert, Shirley. Let My Name Stand Fair. Lippincott,
1956. Light romance of the Revolution in which General Nathanael Greene, Light-Horse Harry Lee, Anthony Wayne, Alexander Hamilton, and George Washington appear.

--- Waters of the Wilderness. Lippincott, 1941. Story of
George Rogers Clark's expeditions in the Ohio wilderness and life in Spanish St. Louis; 1778-1780.

Simons, Katherine. The Red Doe. Appleton, 1953. Exploits of Francis Marion, the Swamp Fox.

Sinclair, Harold. Westward the Tide. Doubleday, 1940.
The war on the frontier; action centers around Fort
Pitt and George Rogers Clark's expedition against
Vincennes.

Singmaster, Elsie. Rifles for Washington. Houghton, 1938.
Story of a young colonist who joins Washington's ragged
army.

Slaughter, Frank. Flight from Natchez. Doubleday, 1955.
Describes the flight of a group of Loyalists from
Natchez in 1781.

Spicer, Bart. Brother to the Enemy. Dodd, 1958. Based
on the attempt of Light-Horse Harry Lee's sergeant-
major, John Champe, to capture Benedict Arnold by
slipping into British occupied New York.

Stanley, Edward. Thomas Forty. Duell, 1947. Follows
the career of a neutral Westchester County journey-
man-printer through the war.

Sterne, Emma Gelders. Drums of the Monmouth. Dodd,
1935. Set in New Jersey and New York. Shows the
part played by the Huguenots and Quakers in the war.
Central character is Philip Freneau.

Swanson, Neil. The Forbidden Ground. Farrar, 1938.
Detroit fur trade at the time of the Revolution.

Taylor, David. Farewell to Valley Forge. Lippincott,
1955. General Charles Lee's plot to betray the colonial forces; the British evacuation of Philadelphia;
and the Battle of Monmouth.

--- Lights Across the Delaware. Lippincott, 1954. Story
of a spirited farm girl torn between her devotion to
the American cause and her pacifist Quaker lover;
centers around Washington's campaign against Trenton;
1776-1777.

--- Storm the Last Rampart. Lippincott, 1960. Adventures of a colonial agent spying on the British in
Tarrytown, New York from the time of Arnold's treason to the surrender of Cornwallis at Yorktown; 1780-

1781.

---   Sycamore Men.  Lippincott, 1958.  The war in South
      Carolina in 1780-1781; Francis Marion, the Swamp
      Fox, fights Cornwallis and Tarleton at the Battles of
      Camden, Kings Mountain, and Eutaw Springs.

Thompson, Maurice.  Alice of Old Vincennes.  Bobbs, 1900.
      Indian warfare and pioneer life in the northwest terri-
      tory in and around Vincennes in 1778.

Turnbull, Agnes.  The Day Must Dawn.  Macmillan, 1942.
      Western Pennsylvania and frontier warfare in the days
      of the Revolution.

Van de Water, Frederick.  Catch a Falling Star.  Duell,
      1949.  Vermont in 1780; story of conflict and divided
      loyalties.

---   Day of Battle.  Washburn, 1958.  Story of the rebel
      forces in Vermont from the Battle of Ticonderoga to
      the Battle of Bennington; 1777.

---   The Reluctant Rebel.  Duell, 1948.  Story of Ethan Allen
      and the Green Mountain boys of New Hampshire; the Bat-
      tle of Ticonderoga; fight over reapportionment of the
      New Hampshire grants.

---   Wings of the Morning.  Washburn, 1956.  Story of
      the struggle for independence and unity in Vermont;
      1774-1791;picture of the political issues involved.

Wheelwright, Jere.  Kentucky Stand.  Scribner, 1951.  A
      Baltimore boy on the Kentucky frontier, 1777, involved
      in politics and frontier warfare.  Daniel Boone, Simon
      Kenton, and Thomas Jefferson appear.

Williams, Ben Ames.  Come Spring.  Houghton, 1940. Life

in a remote Maine settlement during the Revolution.

Wyckoff, Nicholas E. The Braintree Mission. Macmillan,
1957. Based on the idea that England hoped to offer
a title and a seat in Parliament to six colonial leaders
to placate the colonies; this is the story of the offer
made to John Adams.

The Young Nation, 1783 to 1860

The period covered by this category extends from the end of the Revolution to the mid-1800's, thus overlapping in time parts of the two following categories. Novels dealing with the political, social, cultural, and industrial development of the new young nation following the Revolution contribute to a fuller understanding of our history. Some of the themes found in fiction of this period are: the period of Confederation, the ratification of the Constitution, Shays' Rebellion, the Tripolitan War, the War of 1812, the beginnings of industrial and financial development, shipbuilding and the shipping industry, national and local politics in the 1830's and 1840's, musical life in New York in the 1830's, and American literary development in the early 1800's.

Adams, Samuel Hopkins. Banner By the Wayside. Random, 1947. A group of itinerant players tour the Erie Canal country of New York in the 1830's.

--- Canal Town. Random, 1944. Struggles of a young physician fighting ignorance and superstition in New York state in the 1820's; medical lore and customs of the times.

--- The Gorgeous Hussy. Houghton, 1934. Washington social and political life from 1812 to the Civil War; story of Peggy Eaton, protegé of Andrew Jackson.

--- Sunrise to Sunset. Random, 1950. Early days in the shirt-making industry in Troy, New York in the 1830's;

centers around the struggle for better working conditions.

Allis, Marguerite. All In Good Time. Putnam, 1944. Beginnings of American industry at the turn of the century; a Connecticut clockmaker initiates the first steps toward mass production, and faces the hard times of the Embargo Act of 1807.

--- Charity Strong. Putnam, 1945. Picture of the New York musical world in the 1830's.

--- The Law of the Land. Putnam, 1948. Story of the prejudice against public performers in early nineteenth century New England.

--- The Splendor Stays. Putnam, 1942. Social and political developments during the first decades of the nineteenth century; birth of the Monroe Doctrine; Isaac Hull, Simon Bolivar, and others appear; setting is Boston and New York.

--- Water Over the Dam. Putnam, 1947. Story of the fight for the Farmington Canal project in Connecticut in the 1820's.

Bacheller, Irving. Light In the Clearing. Bobbs, 1917. Career of Silas Wright, governor of New York; 1840's and 1850's.

Breslin, Howard. Shad Run. Crowell, 1955. Life of the shad fishermen in the Hudson River valley near Poughkeepsie at the time New York ratified the Constitution in 1788.

--- Tamarack Tree. McGraw, 1947. Story of the affects of a political convention on a small New England town,

Stratton, Vermont, in 1840. William Henry Harrison and Daniel Webster appear.

Caldwell, Janet Taylor. The Wide House. Scribner, 1945. Family story set against a background of social and political developments in a small New York town torn by the conflicts of the "Know-Nothing" party in the 1850's.

Carmer, Carl. Genesee Fever. Farrar, 1941. Background of fairs, horse racing, and political conflict when the Scotch-Irish in the Genesee Valley of New York rebelled against Hamilton's excise law; Colonel Williamson, with Robert Morris and Aaron Burr, planned to establish landed estates in the valley.

Carse, Robert. Great Circle. Scribner, 1956. Story of a whaling voyage out of Salem in the 1840's.

Case, Josephine. Written in Sand. Houghton, 1945. Story of the Tripolitan War, 1801-1805; centering around General Eaton's campaigns in Africa.

Chapman, Maristan (pseud.). Tennessee Hazard. Lippincott, 1953. Tennessee frontier in 1788 in a story of the effort to ratify the Constitution and of General Wilkinson's conspiracy to turn the frontier lands over to the Spanish in Louisiana.

Chase, Mary Ellen. Silas Crockett. Macmillan, 1935. Chronicle of a Maine seafaring family as steam begins to replace sail, and the New England shipbuilding industry declines.

Coatsworth, Elizabeth. Here I Stay. Coward, 1938. Story of Maine in 1817, and the beginning of the rush to the

Ohio wilderness.

Cochran, Louis. The Fool of God. Duell, 1958. Fictional
   biography of the life and times of Alexander Campbell,
   founder of the Disciples of Christ, president of Bethany
   College, and friend of John Brown, Henry Clay, James
   Madison, and Thomas Jefferson.

Coffin, Robert Peter Tristram. John Dawn. Macmillan,
   1936. Maine during the shipbuilding era following the
   Revolution.

Colver, Anne. Listen For the Voices. Farrar, 1939. Concord during the years 1848 to 1851; picture of small
   town life and literary activity; Thoreau, Emerson, and
   the Alcotts mingle with the characters.

Crabb, Alfred Leland. Home to Kentucky. Bobbs, 1953.
   Fictional biography of Henry Clay.

--- Home to the Hermitage. Bobbs, 1948. Story of Andrew and Rachel Jackson, from his return from the
   War of 1812 to the time he leaves for Washington and
   the Presidency.

David, Evan John. As Runs the Glass. Harper, 1943.
   Story of a Maine seafaring family at the time of the
   French revolution.

Davidson, Louis B. and Edward J. Doherty. Captain Mar-
   ooner. Crowell, 1952. Based on an actual mutiny on
   the whaler "Globe" out of Nantucket in 1822.

Davis, Dorothy. Men of No Property. Scribner, 1956.
   Irish immigrants in conflict with the "Know-Nothing"
   faction in New York City in the 1850's.

Degenhard, William. The Regulators. Dial, 1943. Story

of Shay's Rebellion in Massachusetts.

Edmonds, Walter D.  Young Ames.  Little, 1942.  Social,
    political, and economic life in New York City in the
    1830's.

Field, Rachel.  All This and Heaven Too.  Macmillan,
    1938.  Novel of the American literary scene in the
    1850's.  Harriet Beecher Stowe, Samuel Morse, Wil-
    liam Cullen Bryant, and others appear.

Fletcher, Inglis.  The Queen's Gift.  Bobbs, 1952.  Albe-
    marle County, North Carolina in 1788.  Story of the
    debates about the ratification of the Constitution.

Forbes, Esther.  Rainbow on the Road.  Houghton, 1954.
    Story of an itinerant portrait painter in New England
    in the 1830's.

---  The Running of the Tide.  Houghton, 1948.  Novel of
    Salem's great ship building days and the beginning of
    its decline.

Grebenc, Lucile.  The Time of Change.  Doubleday, 1938.
    Customs and daily life of a Connecticut family in the
    years following 1812.

Hackney, Louise.  Wing of Fame.  Appleton, 1934.  Fic-
    tional biography of the founder of the Smithsonian In-
    stitution.  Historical characters are Smithson, Frank-
    lin, Blake, Cavendish, and Lavoisier.

Hawthorne, Nathaniel.  The Blithedale Romance.  1852.
    Story of George Ripley's Brook Farm socialistic ex-
    periment in 1841; associated with the venture were
    Emerson, Hawthorne, Margaret Fuller, and other
    Transcendentalists.

Hergesheimer, Joseph. Balisand. Knopf, 1924. Political developments in Virginia from Washington's second inauguration to Jefferson's election.

--- Java Head. Knopf, 1919. Story of a Salem shipowning family in the 1840's.

Hough, Henry Beetle. The New England Story. Random, 1958. Three generations of a New England whaling family in the 1800's.

Hulme, Kathryn. Annie's Captain. Little, 1961. Story of the long happy marriage of the author's grandparents as a background for the description of the progress from sail to steam in the 1800's.

Idell, Albert. Roger's Folly. Doubleday, 1957. New Jersey, 1844; picture of social and economic life in the period when steam was replacing sail and the railroad empires were being formed. Followed by "Centennial Summer" (Nation Grows Up).

James, Henry. Washington Square. 1881. Social life in New York City in the early 1800's.

Jennings, John. Banners Against the Wind. Little, 1954. Biographical novel of Dr. Samuel Gridley Howe, his interest in the struggle for Greek independence, founding a school for the blind, and marriage to Julia Ward.

--- Salem Frigate. Doubleday, 1946. Adventurous sea story of the early years of the young nation; action centers around the African coast during the Tripolitan War.

Kane, Harnett. New Orleans Woman. Doubleday, 1946. Biographical novel of Myra Clark Gaines and a picture of the New Orleans scene.

Kelland, Clarence Buddington. Hard Money. Harper, 1930.
Son of a Dutch peddler becomes one of the financial
leaders in New York. First in the author's series on
the economic development of the United States (Civil
War and The Nation Grows Up).

Kennedy, Lucy. Mr. Audubon's Lucy. Crown, 1957. Story
of Lucy Bakewell Audubon and of her life with the
naturalist, painter, John James Audubon.

Laing, Alexander. Jonathan Eagle. Duel, 1955. Picture
of American politics from 1786 to 1801; banking poli-
cies of Hamilton, reaction to the Alien and Sedition
Laws, and the election of Jefferson.

---    Mathew Early. Duell, 1957. Story of New England
and the slave trade; heroine is active in a move to
abolish slavery.

LeMay, Alan. Pelican Coast. Doubleday, 1929. New Orleans with its varied characters and the contrast of
sea, town, and river life in the early 1800's.

McKee, Ruth Eleanor. The Lord's Anointed. Doubleday,
1934. Story of the missionaries from Boston who
sailed to Hawaii in 1820.

Malm, Dorothea. The Woman Question. Appleton, 1958.
Amusing novel of the woman's rights movement culminating in a woman's rights convention in New York in
1853. Lucretia Mott, Lucy Stone, and others appear.

Minnigerode, Meade. Cockades. Putnam, 1927. New York
and New Orleans at the time of the French Revolution;
story of the Dauphin's supposed escape to America.

Morrow, Honoré. Black Daniel. Morrow, 1931. Romance
of Daniel Webster and Caroline LeRoy and of her influence on his career.

Muir, Robert. The Sprig of Hemlock. Longmans, 1957.
Story of Shays' Rebellion in Massachusetts in 1786-
1787, when Daniel Shays led an uprising against high
land taxes and debtors prisons.

Murphy, Edward. Angel of the Delta. Hanover, 1958.
Based on the life of Margaret Haughery, who worked
to establish a home for orphan children in New Orleans; follows her struggles during the Union occupation after the Civil War.

O'Neal, Cothburn. The Very Young Mrs. Poe. Crown,
1956. Based on the life of Virginia Clemm, wife of
Edgar Allen Poe; describes the unsettled, emotional
life of the poet and his dependence upon his wife.

O'Neill, Charles. Morning Time. Simon and Schuster,
1949. Based on the supposed plot of General Wilkinson to sell out to the Spanish at New Orleans during
the period of the Confederation, 1783-1789.

Paradise, Viola. Tomorrow the Harvest. Morrow, 1952.
Small town life in Maine just after the Revolution.

Parker, Cornelia Stratton. Fabulous Valley. Putnam, 1956.
Romance set against a background of the oil rush in
Western Pennsylvania in the mid-1800's.

Partridge, Bellamy. The Big Freeze. Crowell, 1948.
Story of the political skulduggery connected with the development of New York's water supply in the 1840's.

Roark, Garland. The Lady and the Deep Blue Sea. Double-

day, 1958. A sea story set around the clipper ship
trade out of Boston; plot revolves around a race from
Melbourne to Boston.

Roberts, Kenneth L. Lydia Bailey. Doubleday, 1947. Story
of Americans in the Haitian revolution and in the Tripolitan War.

Seifert, Shirley. The Three Lives of Elizabeth. Lippincott,
1952. Follows the heroine from her youth on the
Missouri River frontier in the 1820's to maturity as a
leader in Washington society just before the Civil War.

Stone, Irving. The President's Lady. Doubleday, 1951.
Sympathetic account of Rachel and Andrew Jackson
against a background of American politics at the beginning of the nineteenth century.

Seton, Anya. Dragonwyck. Houghton, 1944. Manners and
customs of the early 1800's in a baronial family home
in the Hudson River valley.

Whitney, Janet. Judith. Morrow, 1943.     Philadelphia in
1792 is the background for the love story of two young
people; Washington's second inauguration, Blanchard's
balloon ascent, troubled international relations, and the
yellow fever epidemic are historical high lights.

War of 1812

Banks, Polan. Black Ivory. Harper, 1926. Story of Jean
Lafitte, pirate and slave runner, and of the conflict
involved in his decision to join the Americans in the
defense of New Orleans against the British in the War
of 1812.

Beebe, Ralph. Who Fought and Bled. Coward, 1941. Pi-

oneering in Ohio and General Isaac Hull's campaigns
around Detroit.

Bell, Sallie. Marcel Armand. Page, 1935. Intrigue of
Lafitte's lieutenant with the British.

Chambers, Robert W. The Happy Parrot. Appleton, 1929.
Story of naval warfare during the War of 1812.

--- The Rake and the Hussy. Appleton, 1930. Story of
Jackson's defense of New Orleans.

Chidsey, Donald Barr. Stronghold. Doubleday, 1948.
Connecticut and Martinique during the War of 1812.
Hero is impressed into the British navy.

Finger, Charles. Cape Horn Snorter. Houghton, 1939. New
England shippers in the years leading up to the War of
1812.

Forester, C. S. Captain from Connecticut. Little, 1941.
Blockade running out of Long Island during Jefferson's
administration.

Gordon, Charles William. Rock and the River. Dodd, 1931.
Set in Quebec and on the Canadian-American border
during the War of 1812. Canadian point of view.

--- The Runner. Doubleday, 1929. Fighting around the
Niagara peninsula.

Harper, Robert S. Trumpet in the Wilderness. M.S. Mill,
1940. Story of frontier warfare, the surrender of
Detroit, the Battle of Erie, and pioneer newspaper
work in Ohio.

Hepburn, Andrew. Letter of Marque. Little, 1959. Vivid
account of sea warfare; story of an American privateer

in the War of 1812.

Jennings, John. The Tall Ships. McGraw, 1958. Story of
the American Navy in the period before and during the
War of 1812.

La Farge, Oliver. The Long Pennant. Houghton, 1933.
Rhode Island privateer harrasses British shipping in
the Carribean.

Lane, Carl. The Fleet in the Forest. Coward, 1943. Life
around Erie, Pennsylvania; the building of Perry's
fleet at Presque Isle, and the Battle of Erie.

Lincoln, Joseph Crosby and Freeman Lincoln. The New
Hope. Coward, 1941. Cape Codders launch a privateer through the British blockade.

Marshall, Bernard Gay. Old Hickory's Prisoner. Appleton,
1925. Story of a boy too young to join the army in
the War of 1812 who serves as a messenger, earning
the commendation and a promotion from General Andrew Jackson.

Moore, John. Hearts of Hickory. Cokesbury, 1926. The
defense of New Orleans. Andrew Jackson, David
Crockett, Jean Lafitte.

Mudgett, Helen. The Seas Stand Watch. Knopf, 1944.
Follows the ups and downs of the New England sea
trade and politics from the Revolution through the War
of 1812.

O'Daniel, Janet. O Genesee. Lippincott, 1957. A tale of
pioneer settlers in the Genesee Valley near present
Rochester, New York and the conflicts building up to
the War of 1812.

Orr, Myron. The Citadel of the Lakes. Dodd, 1952. Story
of Astor's fur trading empire around Mackinac Island
during the War of 1812.

Roberts, Kenneth L. Captain Caution. Doubleday, 1934.
Maine merchant ship captured by the British; seamen
impressed into British service.

--- The Lively Lady. Doubleday, 1931. Privateering
against British shipping and life in Dartmoor prison.

Root, Corwin. An American, Sir. Dutton, 1940. Privateering, impressment into British service, and life in
Boston split between Federalists and Republicans during the War of 1812.

Rowland, Henry C. Hirondelle. Harper, 1922. Adventure
on the high seas. Privateering on the eve of the war.

Shepard, Odell and Willard Shepard. Holdfast Gaines. Macmillan, 1946. Panorama of national events from the
end of the Revolution to the War of 1812; includes the
Fort Mims Massacre, Battle of New Orleans; Tecumseh, Jean Lafitte, and Andrew Jackson appear.

Sperry, Armstrong. The Black Falcon. Winston, 1949.
Son of a New Orleans planter sails with Jean Lafitte
in his privateering raids against the English in 1814.

Tracy, Don. Crimson Is the Eastern Shore. Dial, 1953.
The war around the shores of Eastern Maryland.

Williams, Ben Ames. Thread of Scarlet. Houghton, 1939.
Nantucket privateer fights a British frigate during the
War of 1812.

Wilson, Margaret. The Valiant Wife. Doubleday, 1934.
Story of the imprisonment of a young American in

Dartmoor prison in 1812.

Expanding Frontiers, 1783 to 1893

The courses of westward expansion from the Revolution to the closing of the American frontier in the 1890's offers the novelist a multitude of settings, periods, and characters from which to draw: simple tales of family life in a frontier cabin; heroic treks from the East to the wilderness of Western Pennsylvania, Ohio, Kentucky, and Tennessee; fur trade with the Indians and the founding of the cities on the Great Lakes and on the Ohio and Mississippi Rivers; wagon trains pushing westward; the Santa Fe Trail, the Oregon Trail, and the Erie Canal; the War with Mexico; the exodus of the Mormons; the California gold rush; settlement of the plains states; and the development of the Old West. Daniel Boone, Buffalo Bill, General Custer, Aaron Burr, Marcus Whitman, William Bonney, Lewis and Clark, Abraham Lincoln, J.J. Hill, John Jacob Astor, Kit Carson, Santa Anna, David Crockett, and the Indians, Pontiac, Sitting Bull, and Geronimo are among the many historical figures who appear in novels dealing with this phase of American history.

Because of the large number of titles in this group and the variety of themes they cover, they are divided into sections based on the broad geographic areas of our frontier expansion. In general, these areas follow the chronological pattern of the advancing frontier, from "Eastern and Southern Frontiers" through "The Middle West," "The Southwest," "California and the Pacific Northwest," to "The Plains States and the Far West."

Eastern and Southern Frontiers

During the Colonial period the frontier was pushed
slowly inland from the settlements along the Atlantic coast
by hunters and fur traders followed by settlers, until at the
time of the Revolution the Appalachian Mountains had been
breached; the Wautauga and Transylvania settlements had
been made in Tennessee and Kentucky.  George Rogers
Clark's successful expedition against Hamilton in the Northwest Territory and the treaty setting the western boundary
of the United States at the Mississippi River added impetus
to the westward migration.  However, frontier conditions did
not cease to exist as the boundary of the frontier itself ad-
vanced.  The New England states, and Western Pennsylvania
and New York still had areas in which pioneer conditions
existed in the mid-1800's.  In the South, Florida, Georgia,
the Mississippi Territory, and Louisiana furnish abundant
sources for novels of frontier and pioneer life.

Atkinson, Oriana.  The Twin Cousins.  Bobbs, 1951. The
    Catskill country of New York in the days when it was
    still frontier; story of the construction of the Susque-
    hanna Turnpike.

Barnes, Percy Raymond.  Crum Elbow Folks.  Lippincott,
    1938.  Country life and customs of a Quaker settle-
    on the Hudson River in 1838.

Best, Allena.  Homespun.  Lothrop, 1937.  Family life on
    the New York frontier in the 1820's.

Best, Herbert.  Young'un.  Macmillan, 1944.  Picture of
    daily living in the frontier region of Northern New York
    state in the early 1800's.

Boyd, James.  The Long Hunt.  Scribner, 1930.  Life on

the frontier from North Carolina to the Mississippi
River at the time of Daniel Boone.

Bristow, Gwen. Deep Summer. Crowell, 1937. Evolution
of a great Louisiana plantation from a frontier cabin
in the wilderness. Followed by "The Handsome Road"
(Civil War).

Clagett, John. Buckskin Cavalier. Crown, 1954. Story of
a young woman captured by Indians near Fort Pitt;
covers much of the frontier region including a description of the Wilderness Road.

Colver, Anne. Theodosia, Daughter of Aaron Burr. Farrar,
1941. Fictionized biography in which his schemes are
treated casually.

Crabb, Alfred Leland. Journey to Nashville. Bobbs, 1957.
Story of the founding of Nashville, retracing the journey of a group of settlers from the Wautauga Settlement of East Tennessee through the wilderness to the
site of the new town.

Davis, Julia. Eagle On the Sun. Rinehart, 1956. Story of
Virginia plantation life and the Mexican War. Sequel
to "Bridle the Wind" (Civil War - Abolition).

Dowdey, Clifford. Tidewater. Little, 1943. Panoramic
story of the migration from the old Virginia tidewater
plantations to new lands in the West in 1837.

Downes, Anne Miller. The Pilgrim Soul. Lippincott, 1952.
Life in the wilderness area of New Hampshire in 1820.

--- The Quality of Mercy. Lippincott, 1959. Family affairs and politics in Philadelphia and on the Tennessee
frontier at the time of Andrew Jackson's war against

the Creek Indians in 1813.

Edmonds, Walter D.  The Big Barn.  Little, 1930. Story of
farm life in the Black River valley of New York in the
1860's.

---  Chad Hanna.  Little, 1940.  A circus story set in the
Erie Canal region of New York in the 1850's; depicts
the struggle of small business in competition with big
business.

---  Erie Water.  Little, 1933.  Story of the building of the
Erie Canal from 1817 to 1825.

---  Rome Haul.  Little, 1929.  Life and manners along
the banks of the Erie Canal in the 1850's.

---  The Wedding Journey.  Little, 1947.  Story of a honeymoon couple traveling through the Erie Canal on the
way to Buffalo and Niagara Falls in the 1830's.

Forrest, Williams.  Trail of Tears.  Crown, 1958.  Story
of the Cherokee Indians and of their leader, John Ross,
at the time of their enforced migration from their
home in Georgia to new lands in Oklahoma Territory
in the 1830's.

Fort, John.  God In the Straw Pen.  Dodd, 1931.  Story of
a Methodist revival meeting in a Georgia backwoods
community in the 1830's.

Gabriel, Gilbert Wolf.  I Thee Wed.  Macmillan, 1948.
Story of a group who came to America during the
French Revolution to build a refuge for Marie Antoi-
nette at the site of Asylum in Pennsylvania.

Gerson, Noel B.  The Cumberland Rifles.  Doubleday, 1952.
Story of the frontier state of Franklin, its struggle

for recognition, and the admission of Tennessee as a
state in 1796.

Giles, Janice Holt. The Believers. Houghton, 1957. Story
of religious beliefs and social customs of a Shaker
colony in Kentucky in the early 1800's.

--- Land Beyond the Mountains. Houghton, 1958. Story
of the settling of Kentucky from 1783 to 1792 and the
fight for separate statehood, introducing General James
Wilkinson's schemes for an empire on the frontier.

Ham, Tom. Give Us This Valley. Macmillan, 1952. Story
of a Pennsylvania couple moving to new land in a
Georgia valley in 1837.

Harris, Cyril. Street of Knives. Little, 1950. Follows
Aaron Burr's journey westward on his way to Mexico.

Hatcher, Harlan H. The Patterns of Wolfpen. Bobbs, 1934.
Family chronicle from pioneer days in Eastern Kentucky to the encroachment of industry after about 1885.

Holt, Felix. The Gabriel Horn. Dutton, 1951. Frontier
life along the Tennessee River.

Johnson, Gerald White. By Reason of Strength. Minton,
1930. Chronicle of the Campbell clan of North Carolina from just after the Revolution through the Civil
War.

Jones, Madison. Forest of the Night. Harcourt, 1960.
Story of an idealistic school teacher facing the brutal
reality of frontier life in Tennessee in the early 1800's.

Jordan, Mildred. Asylum For the Queen. Knopf, 1948.
Story of a group of aristocrats who plot to rescue the
French Royal family imprisoned in Paris and bring

them to a Pennsylvania colony which they named Asylum.

Kendrick, Baynard H.  The Flames of Time.  Scribner, 1948.  Story of life in Northern Florida preceding its acquisition by the United States.

Kroll, Harry Harrison.  Darker Grows the Valley.  Bobbs, 1947.  Pioneer life in the Tennessee River valley from 1778 to the advent of T.V.A. in the 1930's.

---  Rogue's Companion.  Bobbs, 1943.  Story of John Murrell's outlaw band and life on the Natchez Trace in the 1820's and 1830's.

Loomis, Noel.  The Twilighters.  Macmillan, 1955.  Frontier Kentucky and lands west of the Mississippi River in the early 1800's.

McCutcheon, George B.  Viola Gwyn.  Dodd, 1922.  Frontier Kentucky and Indiana in the early 1800's.

MacKinnon, Mary Linehan.  One Small Candle.  Crown, 1956.  Story of family life in a New York farming community during the mid-1800's.

McMeekin, Clark (pseud.).  Reckon With the River. Appleton, 1941.  Life on the Kentucky frontier and on the Ohio River;  Johnny Appleseed, Aaron Burr, and the Blennerhassetts and others appear.

Markey, Gene.  That Far Paradise.  McKay, 1960. Story of the eventful journey of a Virginia Blue Ridge family to the Kentucky wilderness beyond the Alleghenies in 1794.

Meigs, Cornelia.  Call of the Mountain.  Little, 1940. Vermont backwoods in the 1830's.

Miller, Caroline. Lebanon. Doubleday, 1944. Story of
pioneer life, of hunting and trapping in the Georgia
swamplands and on the Mississippi River frontier.

Myers, John. The Wild Yazoo. Dutton, 1947. Life on
the Mississippi frontier as lived by a Virginia aristo-
crat in the Indian lands above the Yazoo River in the
1780's and 1790's.

Nicholson, Meredith. The Cavalier of Tennessee. Bobbs,
1928. Story of Andrew Jackson, 1789 to 1824; Tennessee in pioneer days.

Pendexter, Hugh. Red Belts. Doubleday, 1920. Story of
the settling of the Tennessee frontier.

--- A Virginia Scout. Bobbs, 1922. Story of Indian warfare on the Virginia frontier.

Poole, Ernest. The Nancy Flyer. Crowell, 1949. A New
Hampshire lad witnesses the end of an era as rail-
roads replace the stagecoach; 1835 through the Civil
War.

Pope, Edith. River in the Wind. Scribner, 1954. Scout-
ing, fighting, and social life in the Florida towns during the Seminole Wars, 1835-1842.

Pridgen, Tim. West Goes the Road. Doubleday, 1944.
Story of a frontiersman fighting Indians, Spaniards,
and Frenchmen for the lands between the Alleghenies
and the Mississippi River, and opposing Wilkinson and
Burr's scheme.

Pryor, Elinor. The Double Man. Norton, 1957. Story of
Indian life on the American frontier and England in the
mid-1800's, as seen by a white man raised by the

Cherokees, educated in England, who returns to live with the Indians.

Roberts, Elizabeth Maddox. The Great Meadow. Viking, 1930. Pioneer life as settlers move from Virginia over the Wilderness Road to Harrod's Fort, Kentucky.

Seton, Anya. My Theodosia. Houghton, 1941. Story of Aaron Burr's daughter, of her relations with her father and his schemes, and of her love for Meriwether Lewis.

Skinner, Constance. Becky Landers, Frontier Warrior. Macmillan, 1926. Story of a pioneer girl on the Kentucky frontier. Daniel Boone and George Rogers Clark appear.

Slaughter, Frank. The Warrior. Doubleday, 1956. The Seminole War of 1835 describing contemporary feeling and the Indian fighting culminating in the capture of Osceola.

Stanley, Edward. The Rock Cried Out. Duell, 1949. The Blennerhassetts develop a homestead on an island in the Ohio River and become involved in Aaron Burr's plot.

Sterne, Emma Gelders. Some Plant Olive Trees. Dodd, 1937. Napoleonic exiles form the Vine and Olive colony at Demopolis, Alabama in the early 1800's.

Street, James. Oh, Promised Land. Dial Press, 1940. Frontier life in the Mississippi Territory (Alabama and Mississippi) from the founding of Natchez to the War of 1812.

Sublette, Clifford and Harry Harrison Kroll. Perilous Jour-

ney.  Bobbs, 1943.  A tale of the Mississippi River
and the Natchez Trace; 1821.

Van Every, Dale.  Captive Witch.  Messner, 1951.  Scout
for George Rogers Clark escorts prisoners from Vincennes to Virginia, then strikes out for new land in
Kentucky.

--- Scarlet Feather.  Holt, 1959.  Story of a Virginia
family who make their way down the Ohio River and
settle in the Kentucky wilderness near Louisville in
1785.

--- The Voyagers.  Holt, 1957.  Life on the frontier in
the 1780's; centers around the Ohio River valley below
Pittsburgh, and the Mississippi River to New Orleans.

--- Westward the River.  Putnam, 1945.  Trip by flatboat
down the Ohio River from Pittsburgh to Louisville in
1794.

Ward, Christopher.  Strange Adventures of Jonathan Drew.
Simon and Schuster, 1932.  Itinerant peddler wanders
through the New England and Middle Western frontier;
1821-1824.  See author's "Yankee Rover" (Expanding
Frontiers - Southwest).

Warren, Robert Penn.  World Enough and Time.  Random,
1950.  Story of a Kentucky murder trial of the 1820's
showing the social and political life of the period.

Welty, Eudora.  The Robber Bridegroom.  Doubleday, 1942.
Fanciful tale of a bandit who steals his bride.  Set in
the Natchez country on the Mississippi River in the
early 1800's.

Wilder, Robert.  Bright Feather.  Putnam, 1948. Fictional

history of the Seminole Wars, 1835-1842. The Seminole leader, Osceola, is one of the characters.

Wylie, I.A.R. Ho, the Fair Wind. Random, 1945. Nar-
row-minded religion versus personal integrity. Setting is Martha's Vinyard at the end of the Civil War.

Young, Stanley. Young Hickory. Farrar, 1940. The early
years of Andrew Jackson from his boyhood in Waxhaw,
North Carolina to his days as a circuit lawyer on the
Tennessee frontier.

## The Middle West

The settlement of the area comprising Ohio, Indiana,
Illinois, Michigan, Wisconsin, Iowa, and Minnesota, has
been treated in a large number of novels covering a wide
range of time from the early settlements on the Ohio River
to the immigration of Norwegians and Irish into Wisconsin
and Minnesota in the 1870's.

Aldrich, Bess Streeter. Song of Years. Appleton, 1939.
Details of home life in pioneer Iowa; 1854-1865.

Allee, Marjorie. A House of Her Own. Houghton, 1934.
Frontier life in Indiana; 1850's and 1860's.

---     Judith Lankester. Houghton, 1930. Story of a Quaker
settlement in Indiana; 1840.

Allis, Marguerite. Brave Pursuit. Putnam, 1954. Story
of the difficulties of acquiring an education on the frontier; set in Southern Ohio. Followed by "The Rising
Storm"(The Civil War-Abolition).

---     Now We Are Free. Putnam, 1952. Story of the westward migration from Connecticut to Ohio just after the Revolution.

--- To Keep Us Free. Putnam, 1953. Development of the Ohio country from 1797 to 1815; settlement at Marietta; founding of Cleveland; the first census; the Burr-Blennerhassett conspiracy; and the War of 1812.

Altrocchi, Julia. Wolves Against the Moon. Macmillan, 1940. Fur trading in the Great Lakes region; 1794-1834.

Atkinson, Eleanor. Hearts Undaunted. Harper, 1917. Story of pioneer hardships in the Middle West, life among the Iroquois Indians, and the founding of Chicago.

Atkinson, Oriana. The Golden Season. Bobbs, 1953. New England sea-faring life and the rush to Ohio in the 1790's.

Auslander, Joseph. My Uncle Jan. Longmans, 1948. Old World customs and festivals among an ebullient family of Czech immigrants in Wisconsin in the 1800's.

Babcock, Bernie. The Soul of Ann Rutledge. Lippincott, 1919. Romance of Abe Lincoln and Ann Rutledge; Illinois from 1831 to 1835.

Bacheller, Irving. Eben Holden. Lothrop, 1900. Story of simple life in the Adirondack Mountain region of New York in the 1850's; introduces Abraham Lincoln and Horace Greeley.

--- A Man for the Ages. Bobbs, 1919. Pioneer days and the formative years of Abraham Lincoln; 1831-1847.

Baldwin, Leland. The Delectable Country. Lee Furman, 1939. Story of the Ohio River keelboat age, the Whiskey Rebellion, and Pittsburgh in the 1790's.

Barney, Helen Corse. Fruit in His Season. Crown, 1951.
Story of a Quaker boy who goes to the Ohio wilderness
a few years after the Revolution.

Benson, Ramsey. Hill Country. Stokes, 1928. Story of
James J. Hill and the settling of the Northwest Minnesota country.

Brigham, Johnson. The Sinclairs of Old Fort Des Moines.
Torch Press, 1927. Pioneer life around Fort Des
Moines, Iowa in the early 1840's; Sioux Indians, boot-
leggers, and squatters.

Brink, Carol. Caddie Woodlawn. Macmillan, 1935. Pioneer Wisconsin in the 1860's.

Colby, Merle. All Ye People. Viking, 1931. Social history of a group of migrants from Vermont to Ohio in
1810.

--- The New Road. Viking, 1933. Traces the development of a settlement on the Maumee River in Ohio
from about 1820 to 1840.

Cook, Roberta St. Clair. The Thing About Clarissa. Bobbs,
1958. Contrasts life in a ladies' seminary in Philadelphia with the manners and customs on the Ohio
frontier in 1837.

Cooper, James Fenimore. The Prairie. Dodd, 1827. Story
of life on the prairies beyond the Mississippi River at
the time of Jefferson's administration. Sequel to "The
Pioneers" (Colonial America).

Daviess, Maria. The Matrix. Century, 1920. The love
story of Nancy Hanks and Thomas Lincoln.

Derleth, August. Bright Journey. Scribner, 1940. Adventures of Hercules Dousman, an agent of John Jacob Astor in the Northwest Territory; 1812-1843.

--- The Hills Stand Watch. Duell, 1960. Pioneer life in a small lead-mining town in Wisconsin in the 1840's; local politics and the movement toward statehood, trouble with the Indians, and details of lead mining.

--- The House on the Mound. Duell, 1958. Continues the story of Hercules Dousman, fur trader and railroad builder, begun in "Bright Journey" (above).

--- Restless Is the River. Scribner, 1939. Story of the early settlement of Wisconsin; 1839-1850.

--- Still Is the Summer Night. Scribner, 1937. Sac Prairie, Wisconsin in the 1880's when lumber rafts were floated down the Wisconsin River.

--- Wind Over Wisconsin. Scribner, 1938. The Black Hawk Wars and the transition from fur trading to farming in Wisconsin in the 1830's.

Duncan, Thomas W. Big River, Big Man. Lippincott, 1959. Story of the Wisconsin logging industry with many characters and with settings in the North woods, New Mexico, New England, and the Civil War South.

Eggleston, Edward. The Circuit Rider. 1874. Daily life and customs and frontier religion in Ohio; 1800-1825.

--- The Hoosier School-Boy. Scribner, 1883. Life in Indiana and Ohio about 1840, showing the difficulties of acquiring an education on the frontier.

--- The Hoosier School-Master. Scribner, 1871. Tale of Indiana backwoods life and education in the 1850's.

--- The Graysons. Scribner, 1887. Picture of daily life
and customs in rural Illinois about 1850.

Ellis, William D. The Bounty Lands. World, 1952. Story
of conflict between speculators and settlers in Ohio
after the Revolution involving lands granted to the veterans for their war service.

--- The Brooks Legend. Crowell, 1958. Story of medical
practice and daily life on the Ohio frontier in the years
following the War of 1812; continues the story of some
of the characters of "The Bounty Lands" (above).

--- Jonathan Blair, Bounty Lands Lawyer. World, 1954.
Story of a lawyer on the Ohio frontier; picture of daily
life and customs; sequel to "The Bounty Lands."

Faralla, Dana. Circle of Trees. Lippincott, 1955. Story
of the prairies of Minnesota in 1880, and of the Danes
who settle there.

Finney, Gertrude E. The Plums Hang High. Longmans,
1955. Story of family life on a pioneer farm in the
American Midwest; 1868 to 1890.

Fuller, Iola. The Loon Feather. Harcourt, 1940. Fictionized autobiography of Tecumseh's daughter. Setting
is the Mackinac region in the early 1800's.

--- The Shining Trail. Duell, 1943. Centers around the
life of the Sauk Indians and their struggles leading up
to the Black Hawk Wars; 1820's to the 1830's.

Garth, David. Fire on the Wind. Putnam, 1951. Story of
the Upper Michigan penisula in the 1860's; logging,
mining, and railroading.

Gay, Margaret Cooper. Hatchet in the Sky. Simon and

Schuster, 1954. Life with the Ojibway Indians under Chief Pontiac in the Northwest Territory; scenes in early Detroit.

Hallet, Richard. Michael Beam. Houghton, 1939. Story of the Black Hawk War and life on the Illinois and Wisconsin frontier; 1820's and 1830's.

Harris, Laura B. Bride of the River. Crowell, 1956. Story of the adjustment of a Louisiana plantation belle to life in a small Ohio River town in the late 1830's, including slave traffic on the Underground Railroad.

Havill, Edward. Big Ember. Harper, 1947. Norwegian immigrants and the uprising of the Sioux in Southern Minnesota in 1862.

Havighurst, Walter. Quiet Shore. Macmillan, 1937. Homesteading on Lake Erie just after the Civil War, and the growth of industry in Ohio.

--- Winds of Spring. Macmillan, 1940. The settling of Wisconsin; 1840's to 1870's.

Kantor, MacKinlay. Spirit Lake. World, 1961. Story of the settlers and the Indians involved in the Spirit Lake massacre in Iowa in 1857; picture of social and economic life on the frontier in the 1850's.

Krause, Herbert. The Oxcart Trail. Bobbs, 1954. Story of settlers and traders pushing into the Minnesota Territory in the 1850's.

Lancaster, Bruce. For Us the Living. Stokes, 1940. Abraham Lincoln in Indiana and Illinois.

Lockwood, Sarah. Fistful of Stars. Appleton, 1947. Northern Wisconsin in the 1880's.

Lovelace, Maud Hart.  The Black Angels.  Day, 1926.
Story of a musical family touring small towns of the
Minnesota Territory; local color and social history.

--- Early Candlelight.  Day, 1929.  Frontier life along
the Minnesota and the Mississippi Rivers; Fort Snel-
ling (St. Paul), Minnesota in the 1830's.

--- and D. W. Lovelace.  Gentlemen from England.  Macmillan, 1937.  Picture of life in Minnesota; 1860's -
1870's.

--- One Stayed at Welcome.  Day, 1934.  Pioneering in
Minnesota in the 1850's.

Lutes, Della.  Gabriel's Search.  Little, 1940.  Details of
daily life in Michigan in the early 1800's.

McLean, Sydney.  Moment of Time.  Putnam, 1945. Seventy
years in the life of a pioneer woman from girlhood
before the Revolution to the 1840's.

MacLeod, LeRoy.  The Years of Peace.  Appleton, 1932.
Story of daily life in the Wabash River valley of Indiana after the Civil War.

McNeil, Everett.  Daniel DuLuth.  Dutton, 1926.  Story of
the exploration of the Great Lakes from Montreal to
Lake Superior by Daniel DuLuth.

Masters, Edgar Lee.  Children of the Market Place.  Macmillan, 1922.  Story of an English immigrant in Illinois; 1833-1861.

Matshat, Cecile Hulse.  Preacher on Horseback.  Farrar,
1940.  Story of a circuit-riding preacher in Michigan
and Northern New York in the 1870's.

Meader, Stephen.  Boy with a Pack.  Harcourt, 1939. Tale

of a young itinerant peddler wandering from New
Hampshire to the Ohio frontier, 1837.

Means, Florence. Candle in the Mist. Houghton, 1931.
Minnesota in the 1870's.

Meigs, Cornelia. Swift Rivers. Little, 1932. Minnesota in
the early 1800's. Floating logs down the Mississippi
River to St. Louis.

Miller, Helen Topping. Born Strangers. Bobbs, 1949.
Picture of life in Michigan from pioneer days to the
Civil War.

Moberg, Vilhelm. The Last Letter Home. Simon and Schuster, 1961. Picture of the growth of frontier communities in the Minnesota Territory, the Sioux uprising and the Civil War, and details of family life up
to 1890. Sequel to "Unto a Good Land" (below).

--- Unto a Good Land. Simon and Schuster, 1954. Story
of Swedish immigrants pioneering in the Minnesota
Territory in the 1850's.

Orr, Myron David. Mission to Mackinac. Dodd, 1956.
Story of English-French conflict in the area of Mackinac Island prior to the War of 1812.

Oskison, John. Brothers Three. Macmillan, 1935. Farm
life in the Indian Territory after 1873.

Ostenso, Martha. O River, Remember. Dodd, 1943. I-
rish and Norwegian pioneers in the Red River valley
of the Minnesota country; 1870-1941.

Peattie, Donald Culross. A Prairie Grove. Simon and
Schuster, 1938. Saga of missionaries, traders, Indians, settlers, and the founding of Chicago.

Quick, Herbert. The Hawkeye. Bobbs, 1923. Political,
    social, and farm life in Iowa, 1857-1878. Sequel to
    "Vandemark's Folly."

--- Vandemark's Folly. Bobbs, 1922. Pioneering in
    Iowa, 1840's to 1860's; claim jumping, frontier law,
    and the Underground Railroad.

Reed, Warren. She Rode a Yellow Stallion. Bobbs, 1950.
    Farming and horse raising in Southeastern Wisconsin,
    1840's - 1890's; picture of German, Irish, and Scottish
    settlers and the development of the cheese industry.

Richter, Conrad. The Fields. Knopf, 1946. Story of the
    development of a community in the Ohio wilderness.

--- The Town, Knopf, 1950. Emergence of a frontier
    town and the trappings of civilization in the Ohio wil-
    derness.

--- The Trees. Knopf, 1940. First of a
    series on the development of the Ohio wilderness.
    Followed by "The Fields" and "The Town" (see above).

Seifert, Shirley. The Wayfarer. M.S. Mill, 1938. Fic-
    tional biography of John Cotter; whaling, trading in the
    West, fighting in the Civil War, and stock farming in
    Missouri.

Selby, John. Elegant Journey. Rinehart, 1944. Southerner
    frees slaves and starts out anew in Wisconsin; 1840's.

Sinclair, Harold. American Years. Doubleday, 1938. His-
    tory of a small Illinois town; 1830 to the Civil War.

Snedeker, Caroline. Beckoning Road. Doubleday, 1929.
    Story of the New Harmony settlement in Indiana in the
    1840's.

--- Seth Way. Houghton, 1917. The New Harmony settlement in Indiana in the 1840's.

--- The Town of the Fearless. Doubleday, 1931. European background and the founding of the New Harmony community in Indiana. Robert Owen, Pestalozzi, and others appear.

Spicer, Bart. The Wild Ohio. Dodd, 1953. Settlement of French emigres at Gallipolis, Ohio.

Stong, Philip. Buckskin Breeches. Farrar, 1937. Westward migration from Ohio to Iowa, 1837.

Suchow, Ruth. Country People. Knopf, 1924. Family chronicle of pioneer hardships of a group of German-Americans who settled in Iowa in the 1850's.

Swanson, Neil. The Phantom Emperor. Putnam, 1934. Based on an attempt to form a separate empire in the Northwest Territory in 1836.

Teilhet, Darwin. Steamboat on the River. Sloane, 1952. Story of the first steamboat on the Sangamon River in Illinois in the 1830's; introduces Abe Lincoln, who pilots the boat to safety around New Salem.

Titus, Harold. Black Feather. Macrae, 1936. Story of the Astor fur trading enterprise around Mackinac Island.

Todd, Helen. So Free We Seem. Reynal, 1936. Story of a pioneer woman on the Missouri frontier.

Troyer, Howard. The Salt and the Savor. Wyn, 1950. Chronicles the development of Indiana from pioneer days to the Civil War; development of the Grange movement, daily life and customs.

Van Every, Dale. The Trembling Earth. Messner, 1953.
Lead mining in Southeast Missouri at the time of the
New Madrid earthquake of 1811.

West, Jessamyn. The Friendly Persuasion. Harcourt,
1945. Episodes in the life of a Quaker family in Indiana, including a minor Civil War encounter.

Whitlock, Brand. The Strangers on the Island. Appleton,
1933. Story of the exiled group of Mormons on Beaver
Island in Lake Michigan in 1850.

Wilson, Margaret. Able McLaughlins. Harper, 1923. Midwestern Scotch community in the 1860's.

Wyckoff, Nicholas. The Corinthians. Macmillan, 1960.
Story of small town life in Illinois and Missouri in the
1850's; pictures the effect of the Mormons on the
places and people they meet on their westward movement.

Zara, Louis. This Land Is Ours. Houghton, 1940. Story
of American frontier life from the Susquehanna to the
Mississippi River, 1755 to 1835; Chief Pontiac, George
Rogers Clark, and General Anthony Wayne appear.


The Southwest
        The history of the American Southwest - Texas, New
Mexico, Arizona, and Oklahoma - can be summed up in a
relatively few subjects as far as historical fiction is concerned:  the struggle for Texas independence and the siege
of the Alamo; the Mexican War; life along the Sante Fe
Trail; conflict with the Indians; Indian life and customs;
cattlemen versus homesteaders; and outlaws and characters.

Adams, Andy. Log of a Cowboy. Houghton, 1903. Picture of Western ranch life; daily journal of a cattle drive from Texas to Wyoming.

Arnold, Elliot. Blood Brother. Duell, 1947. Account of the Apache wars in New Mexico and Arizona; sympathetic with the Indians.

--- Time of the Gringo. Knopf, 1953. Story of New Mexico under the Mexican governor, Don Manuel Armijo, just before the Mexican War.

Aydelotte, Dora. Run of the Stars. Appleton, 1940. Picture of life in the Oklahoma Territory at the time of its settlement in the 1890's.

--- Trumpets Calling. Appleton, 1938. Story of the Cherokee Strip and the settling of Oklahoma in the 1890's.

Baker, Karle. Star of the Wilderness. Coward, 1942. Story of the struggle for Texas independence; set chiefly in Nacagdoches.

Barrett, Monte. The Tempered Blade. Bobbs, 1946. Fictional biography of James Bowie from 1815 to his death at the Alamo in 1836.

Bean, Amelia. The Feud. Doubleday, 1960. Violent story of sheep and cattle ranching, based on the Graham-Tewksbury feud in Arizona in the 1880's.

Bennett, Dwight. Cherokee Outlet. Doubleday, 1961. Opening of the Cherokee Strip in Northern Oklahoma in 1893; shows the change from open prairie to farm land and the development of towns.

Blacker, Irwin R. Taos. World, 1959. Revolt of the Pueb-

lo Indians against the Spaniards in New Mexico in
1680; climaxed by the bloody massacre at Santa Fe.

Blake, Forrester. Johnny Christmas. Morrow, 1948. A-
merican Southwest from 1836 to 1846, when Mexicans
opposed the incoming Americans.

Bosworth, Allan Bernard. The Long Way North. Doubleday, 1959. Story of character played out during a
cattle drive from Texas to Montana Territory.

Boyd, James. Bitter Creek. Scribner, 1939. Incidents of
ranch life and Indian warfare in the story of a young
boy making his way to the West in the 1870's.

Brand, Max. The Long Chance. Dodd, 1941. The Old
West in the days before the Civil War.

Bristow, Gwen. Jubilee Trail. Crowell, 1950. Story of
a trading and honeymoon trip over the Santa Fe Trail
from New York to California in 1845.

Brown, Dee. Wave High the Banner. Macrae, 1942. The
life of Davy Crockett, from boyhood to death at the
Alamo.

Burnett, William Riley. Adobe Walls. Knopf, 1953. Story
of the last Apache uprising in the 1880's and of the
tactics used by Generals Crook and Miles in defeating
the Indians.

--- Mi, Amigo. Knopf, 1959. Based on the Lincoln
County wars in New Mexico in 1878 and the story of
Billy the Kid (William Bonney).

--- Saint Johnson. Longmans, 1930. Story of lawless
Tombstone, Arizona and the Earp-Clanton feud.

Busch, Niven. Duel in the Sun. Morrow, 1944. Texas in
the 1880's with wide-open towns and cattlemen fighting
the railroad and the homesteaders.

Campbell, Walter Stanley. Dobe Walls. Houghton, 1929.
Life on the Santa Fe Trail in the days of Kit Carson.

Cather, Willa. Death Comes For the Archbishop. Knopf,
1927. Story of two French priests in New Mexico
soon after the Mexican War.

Comfort, Will. Apache. Dutton, 1931. Story of Mangus
Colorado, famous Apache chieftain, and of his efforts
to unite the Indians.

Constant, Alberta. Oklahoma Run. Crowell, 1955. Pioneer
life and homesteading in the Oklahoma Territory in the
1890's.

Cook, Will. Elizabeth By Name. Dodd, 1958. Life on a
frontier trading post on the Texas prairie in the post-
Civil War period.

Cooke, David Coxe. The Post of Honor. Putnam, 1958.
Authentic picture of Indian-white relations and details
of Apache Indian fighting on an isolated outpost in the
Arizona Territory.

Cooper, Courtney Ryley. Oklahoma. Little, 1926. Epic
tale of the opening of the Oklahoma Territory to homesteading, the rush of settlers, and the development of
the state.

Corle, Edwin. Billy the Kid. Duell, 1953. Fictional biography of the famous outlaw, William Bonney.

Culp, John H. Born Of the Sun. Sloane, 1959. Life on
a Texas cattle ranch in the 1870's; picture of the cattle

drives to Kansas.

--- The Men of Gonzales. Sloane, 1960. Story of the
hurried march of 32 men from Gonzales to San Antonio in 1836 to reinforce the besieged garrison at the
Alamo.

Davis, James F. The Road to San Jacinto. Bobbs, 1936.
Sam Houston and the struggle for Texas independence;
1835-1836. Bowie, Crockett, and Travis appear.

Dodge, Louis. The American. Messner, 1934. Saga of
the American West in the 1850's; the gold rush, homesteading, fur trading, fighting the Indians, and life on
the Santa Fe Trail.

Duffus, Robert L. Jornada. Covici, 1935. A romance of
the Southwest; wagon trains to Sante Fe; Indian raids;
and the Mexican War.

Erdman, Loula. The Edge of Time. Dodd, 1950. Story
of a wagon journey to the Texas panhandle and life on
an isolated farm on the prairie in 1885.

--- The Far Journey. Dodd, 1955. Overland trip from
Missouri to Texas in the 1890's.

Evarts, Hal. Tumbleweeds. Little, 1923. The Cherokee
Strip and the Oklahoma frontier in the 1890's.

Ferber, Edna. Cimarron. Doubleday, 1930. Oklahoma
from the opening of the Cherokee Strip in the 1890's
to the striking of oil; picture of the development of
the state.

Fergusson, Harvey. The Conquest of Don Pedro. Morrow,
1954. Social history of a frontier town in New Mexico
soon after the Civil War.

--- In Those Days. Knopf, 1929. Story of the development of a small town on the Rio Grande River from
the days of wagon trains and Indian raids to the 1920's.

Foreman, Leonard. The Road to San Jacinto. Dutton,
1943. Story of Davy Crockett on the way to join the
Texans in defense of the Alamo.

Gerson, Noel B. The Golden Eagle. Doubleday, 1953.
The Mexican War, 1845-1848; secret agent draws maps
of Vera Cruz for General Winfield Scott.

Giles, Janice Holt. Johnny Osage. Houghton, 1960. Story
of a young trader living among the Osage Indians in
Oklahoma Territory in the 1820's.

--- Savanna. Houghton, 1961. Story of a woman facing
life alone in Arkansas Territory in the 1830's; plot
involves competition between trading posts around Fort
Gibson and the activities of Sam Houston.

Gipson, Fred. Old Yeller. Harper, 1956. Boy life on a
prairie farm in Texas in the 1860's.

Glidden, Frederick. And the Wind Blows Free. Macmillan,
1945. Story of the cattlemen evicted from the Indian
grasslands, later a part of Oklahoma, by order of
President Cleveland in the 1880's.

Gorman, Herbert. The Wine of San Lorenzo. Farrar,
1945. Presents the Mexican viewpoint of the Mexican
War; an American boy, captured at the Alamo, fights
with Santa Anna in the war.

Grant, Blanch. Dona Lona. Funk, 1941. Santa Fe and
Taos, New Mexico in the 1830's and 1840's.

Grey, Zane. Fighting Caravans. Harper, 1929. The West

at the time of the Civil War.

--- The Heritage of the Desert. Harper, 1910. Mormons,
Indians, and cowboys in a story of life on the Arizona
desert during the early days of the settlement of the
Southwest.

Hall, Oakley. Warlock. Viking, 1958. Story of the violent life in a frontier mining town in the Southwest
Territory in the 1880's.

Hogan, Pendleton. The Dark Comes Early. Washburn,
1934. Events leading up to the fight for Texas independence and to the Mexican War.

Hooker, Forrestine. When Geronimo Rode. Doubleday,
1924. Life in a frontier army post during the last
campaign against the Apache Indians in Arizona.

Horgan, Paul. A Distant Trumpet. Farrar, 1960. Life
on a remote army post, Fort Delivery, in the Arizona Territory in the 1880's in the face of constant
threat of attack by the Apaches.

Hough, Emerson. North of 36. Appleton, 1923. Story of
the beginnings of the great cattle drives from Texas
north to the railroad markets in Kansas.

Houston, Margaret Bell. Cottonwoods Grow Tall. Crown,
1958. Family life and tragedy on a Texas ranch in
the 1890's.

James, Will. The American Cowboy. Scribner, 1942.
Picture of cattle ranching in the Southwest, through
three generations of cowhands.

Jennings, John. Shadows in the Dusk. Little, 1955. A
tale of Apache revenge for the plot of unscrupulous

whites to collect the government bounty on Indian
scalps; picture of copper mining in the Southwest.

Kelland, Clarence Buddington. Valley of the Sun. Harper,
1940. Tale of Arizona and the beginnings of Phoenix
in the 1870's.

Kirkland, Elithe. Divine Average. Little, 1952. Theme
of racial tolerance and the conflict between Americans,
Indians, and Mexicans in Texas in 1838.

--- Love is a Wild Assault. Doubleday, 1959. Daily life,
politics, and brutality in early Texas; a biographical
novel based on the life of Harriet Ann Moore, a Texas
pioneer.

Krey, Laura. On the Long Tide. Houghton, 1940. Story
of the American settlement of Texas, 1812-1836; Sam
Houston, Stephen Austin, Bill Travis, Andrew Jackson,
and others appear.

Lanham, Edwin. The Wind Blew West. Longmans, 1935.
Political, economic, and social development of a small
Texas town from 1875 to 1885.

Laughlin, Ruth. The Wind Leaves No Shadow. Whittlesey,
1948. Santa Fe in the years before the Mexican War.

Lea, Tom. The Wonderful Country. Little, 1952. Story
of the people who helped build Puerto, Texas in the
1880's; includes Texas Rangers, railroad promotors,
Mexicans, and Indians.

LeMay, Alan. The Searchers. Harper, 1954. Life on the
Texas frontier just after the Civil War when the Comanches were opposing encroachment by white settlers.

--- The Unforgiven. Harper, 1957. Pioneer life under

the threat of a Kiowa Indian attack in Texas in the 1870's.

Loomis, Noel. A Time For Violence. Macmillan, 1960. Story of the struggles between ranchers and outlaws in the Texas panhandle in the 1880's.

McCarter, Margaret. Vanguards of the Plains. Harper, 1917. Story of an expedition from Kansas City to Santa Fe in the 1840's.

Mulford, Clarence E. Bring Me His Ears. McClurg, 1922. Adventures on the Missouri River and the Santa Fe Trail in the 1840's.

Newsom, Ed. Wagons To Tucson. Little, 1954. Story of a wagon train crossing the plains to Arizona at the close of the Civil War; picture of Apache raids and life at Fort Reno in Oklahoma Territory.

Ogden, George Washington. The Land of Last Chance. Mc Clurg, 1919. Story of the land run and the settling of the Oklahoma Territory in the 1890's.

--- Sooner Land. Dodd, 1929. Story of pioneering and homesteading in Oklahoma Territory in the 1890's.

O'Meary, Walter. Spanish Bride. Putnam, 1954. The Spanish struggling to maintain control in the Southwest; story of the mistress of the Spanish governor in Santa Fe.

O'Rourke, Frank. Far Mountains. Morrow, 1959. An orphan Irish-American boy grows up as a Spanish-Mexican in Taos, New Mexico; story of the decline of Spanish influence, culminating in the U. S. annexation of Texas and the invasion of Mexico during the Mexican

War; 1801 - 1848.

Oskison, John Milton.  Black Jack Davy.  Appleton, 1926.
Story of life among pioneer settlers who move from
Arkansas to the Indian territory of the Southwest in the
1800's.

Pearce, Richard.  The Impudent Rifle.  Lippincott, 1951.
Life in a frontier fort in the Arkansas Territory during the Jackson administration; pictures the migration
of the Choctaws, and war with the Comanches.

--- The Restless Border.  Lippincott, 1953.  Comanche
warfare and fights with Santa Anna at an army outpost
on the Red River in the 1840's.

Prebble, John.  The Buffalo Soldiers.  Harcourt, 1959.
Story of a patrol of Negro recruits accompanying a
group of Comanches on their last buffalo hunt.

--- Spanish Stirrup.  Harcourt, 1958.  Story of one of
the first great cattle drives from Texas to market in
Kansas, depicting hardships of the drive and the savage
attack of the Comanches.

Putnam, George Palmer.  Hickory Shirt.  Duell, 1949.
Story of the hazards encountered by a wagon train
struggling through Death Valley.

Richter, Conrad.  The Lady.  Knopf, 1957.  Tale of violence and revenge in the Spanish-American society of
Northern New Mexico in the 1880's.

--- Tacey Cromwell.  Knopf, 1942.  Daily life and society
in a frontier mining town in Arizona in the 1890's;
pictures the importance of miners and bankers in the
life of the mining towns of the period.

Seifert, Shirley. Destiny in Dallas. Lippincott, 1958.
Story of Alexander and Sarah Cockrell, centering
around their part in the early development of Dallas,
Texas; 1858.

--- The Turquoise Trail. Lippincott, 1950. Overland from
Independence, Missouri to Santa Fe in 1846.

Shelton, Jess. Hangman's Song. Chilton, 1960. Story of
family pride and revenge set in frontier Missouri,
Arkansas, and Indian Territory in the 1850's.

Smith, William Fielding. Diamond Six. Doubleday, 1958.
Fictional biography of Wesley Smith, Texas Ranger,
Southern soldier in the Civil War, Indian fighter, sher-
iff, and owner of the Diamond Six ranch.

Taylor, Ross. The Saddle and the Plow. Bobbs, 1942.
Conflict between cattlemen and farmers in Texas in
the 1880's.

Thomason, John. Gone to Texas. Scribner, 1937. Danger
and excitement in a fort on the Rio Grande River after
the Civil War.

Venable, Clarke. All the Brave Rifles. Reilly and Lee,
1929. Life in Tennessee, in Washington, and in Texas
and the events leading up to the war for Texas independence; fall of the Alamo; Santa Anna, Sam Houston,
David Crockett, and others appear.

Ward, Christopher. Yankee Rover. Simon and Schuster,
1932. Itinerant New England peddler wanders through
the Southwest; 1824-1829. See also "The Strange Adventures of Jonathan Drew" (Expanding Frontiers-
Eastern and Southern).

Ward, John. Don't You Cry For Me. Scribner, 1940.
Story of the American West; 1846-1847.

Wellman, Paul. Broncho Apache. Macmillan, 1936. Story
of Massai, one of Geronimo's warriors, captured and
sent to a Florida prison after Geronimo's surrender,
and of his escape and revenge.

---   The Comancheros. Doubleday, 1952. A New Orleans
gambler becomes Texas Ranger and tracks down Comancheros leading Indians in attacks against settlers
on the Texas border.

---   The Iron Mistress. Doubleday, 1951. Fictionized
biography of James Bowie.

---   Ride the Red Earth. Doubleday, 1958. Set in the
Southwest and Mexico in the early 1700's at the time
of the struggle between France and Spain for the Texas
territory; pictures Louis Juchereau de St. Denis' role
in the struggle.

Wormser, Richard Edward. Battalion of Saints. McKay,
1960. Story of a battalion of Mormons from Council
Bluffs, Iowa who march to New Mexico to join the U.
S. troops in the Mexican War in 1846.


California and the Pacific Northwest

California and Oregon became states in 1850 and 1858,
respectively, thus being in the position of outposts separated
from the rest of the United States by the Great American
Desert, a vast expanse of mountains and plains considered
unfit for white habitation, and it was to these outposts that
pioneers looked for land to settle before turning to the

plains for their rich soil and to the mountains for their rich
mineral deposits. Episodes in the history of this region
have dealt with novels centering around Spanish life and missionary activities in Mexico and California, the California gold rush
and politics leading to statehood, the Lewis and Clark explorations, establishment of the early fur trading outposts and
the settlement of Oregon, the British-American boundary
dispute, and early Russian efforts to colonize the Northwest.

Ainsworth, Edward. Eagles Fly West. Macmillan, 1946.
Picture of New York and California in the 1840's and
1850's; story of a newspaperman who takes part in
the fighting between U.S. troops and Spanish Californians; the discovery of gold, and the struggle for
statehood.

Allen, T. D. (pseud.). Doctor in Buckskin. Harper, 1951.
Story of Marcus and Narcissa Whitman among the Indians in Oregon and the Northwest.

Bartlett, Lanier. Adios! Morrow, 1929. California just
after the American acquisition in 1846, when a band
of desperados refuse to recognize U. S. control and
harass the settlers.

Beach, Rex. The World In His Arms. Putnam, 1946.
Competition between Russian and American sealers off
Alaska; scenes in Russian Alaska and in San Francisco.

Bedford, Donald (pseud.) John Barry. Creative Age, 1947.
Hero rises from clerk to financier and prominent
citizen; the gold rush starts, and Yerba Buena becomes
San Francisco.

Berry, Don. Trask. Viking, 1960. Story of the first
homesteaders in the Oregon Territory in the 1840's,

and of their troubles with the Indians.  Based on the
life of Elbridge Trask, an early settler.

Binns, Archie.  The Headwaters.  Duell, 1957.  Story of a
young couple struggling against the hardships of pioneering in the wilderness of the Northwest in the 1890's.

--- Mighty Mountain.  Scribner, 1940.  Story of pioneer
hardships in Washington in the 1850's and of the campaigns against the Indians.

--- You Rolling River.  Scribner, 1947.  Life in the port
town of Astoria at the mouth of the Columbia River
about 1865.

Bretherton, Vivien.  Rock and the Wind.  Dutton, 1942.
Frontier life of the early settlers in the Pacific
Northwest, and the development of the area with the
coming of the railroad.

Cameron, Margaret.  Johndover.  Harper, 1924.  Pictur-
esque details of life in California at the time of the
gold rush.

Campbell, Patricia.  The Royal Anne Tree.  Macmillan,
1956.  Romantic novel set on an isolated homestead
in Washington Territory in the 1850's.

Case, Victoria.  The Quiet Life of Mrs. General Lane.
Doubleday, 1952.  Fictionized biography of Polly and
Joseph Lane.  Contrasts Polly's life at home raising
ten children with that of General Lane in the legisla-
ture, the Mexican War, and fighting for statehood for
Oregon.

Coolidge, Dane.  Gringo Gold.  Dutton, 1939.  Life of the
Mexican bandit, Joaquin Murrietta; a story of Califor-

nia in the gold rush days of 1849.

Cranston, Paul. To Heaven on Horseback. Messner, 1952.
Based on the lives of Narcissa and Marcus Whitman,
missionaries and pioneers in Oregon in the 1830's.

Davis, Harold Lenoir. The Distant Music. Morrow, 1957.
Poetic story of the development of the Columbia River
country in Washington Territory from wilderness to
settled country, and the founding of towns.

Elwood, Muriel. Against the Tide. Bobbs, 1950. Los
Angeles in 1879. Conflict between the old Spanish
heritage and the new American ways.

Emmons, Della. Sacajawea of the Shoshones. Binfords
and Mort, 1943. Fictional account of the life of the
Shoshone woman who guided Lewis and Clark, from
her childhood to later years in St. Louis and her return to the reservation.

Evarts, Hal. Fur Brigade. Little, 1928. Story of fur
trading in the Northwest; 1815-1835.

Fisher, Vardis. Tale of Valor. Doubleday, 1958. Story
of the Lewis and Clark expedition.

Footner, Hulbert. The Furbringers. McCann, 1920. Fur
trading in the Northwest.

Gabriel, Gilbert Wolf. I, James Lewis. Doubleday, 1932.
Story of John Jacob Astor's trading post expedition to
the Pacific Northwest in 1810-1811; founding of
Astoria; massacre of the crew of the "Tonquin."

Hargreaves, Sheba. The Cabin At the Trail's End. Harper,
1928. Indian customs and pioneer life during a family's first year in Oregon; 1843-1844.

Haycox, Ernest. The Adventurers. Little, 1954. Picture
of colonization of the Northwest; Oregon in the mid-
1860's; development of the lumber industry.

--- The Earthbreakers. Little, 1952. Story
of settlers in the Oregon Territory, 1845.

Hough, Emerson. 54-40 or Fight. Bobbs, 1909. Story of
the political and personal conflicts behind the Northwest boundary treaty and the annexation of Texas;
introduces the English minister, Pakenham, John C.
Calhoun, and the Russian Baroness von Ritz in major
roles.

Hueston, Ethel. Star of the West. Bobbs, 1935. Story of
the Lewis and Clark expedition of 1803-1806.

Jackson, Helen Hunt. Ramona, 1884. Story of relations
between Indians and Spanish-Mexicans in California at
the time of the American conquest.

Jennings, John. River to the West. Doubleday, 1948.
Dangers of frontier exploration contrasted with the picture of New York society in the days of John Jacob
Astor and his friend Washington Irving; centers around
the Astor fur trading scheme in the Northwest; 1808-
1811.

Jones, Edwal. Vermillion. Prentice, 1947. A hundred
years of California history centered in the story of
the Five Apostles mine started in 1846.

Jones, Nard. Swift Flows the River. Dodd, 1940. Oregon
and the Columbia River region, 1856.

Kyne, Peter B. Tide of Empire. Cosmopolitan, 1928.
California during the gold rush.

MacDonald, William. California Caballero. Covici, 1936. California in the late 1860's when the Americans were supplanting the old Spanish families.

McKee, Ruth Eleanor. Christopher Strange. Doubleday, 1941. Easterner makes overland trip from Concord to San Francisco in the 1850's. Pictures political corruption, vigilantes, and life on an old Spanish ranch.

McNeilly, Mildred. Each Bright River. Morrow, 1950. Oregon in 1845. South Carolina girl goes to Oregon, finds her sweetheart dead, and adjusts to frontier life.

--- Heaven Is Too High. Morrow, 1944. Russian America in the days when Aleksandr Baranov was seeking to open the Pacific Northwest to the Russian fur trade and to establish colonies there; 1780-90's.

Marshall, Edison. Seward's Folly. Little, 1924. Romance built around the purchase of Alaska by the U. S. in 1867.

Miller, May. First the Blade. Knopf, 1938. First part set in Missouri during the Civil War; second part deals with settling in the San Joaquin Valley in California. Coming of the railroad, and digging irrigation ditches.

Morrow, Honoré. Beyond the Blue Sierra. Morrow, 1932. Story of Juan de Anza and the first overland route from Mexico to the Spanish colony at the site of San Francisco.

--- We Must March. Stokes, 1925. Marcus Whitman crossing the Rockies.

Norris, Kathleen. Certain People of Importance. Doubleday, 1922. Fictional history of the life and times of

San Francisco; the days of the gold rush, Spanish
ranch life, growth of the tea and spice business, and
the development of the city.

O'Dell, Scott. Hill of the Hawk. Bobbs, 1947. Story of
California under Spanish rule about the time Captain
Fremont led the Americans in the conquest of the
territory.

Older, Cora. Savages and Saints. Dutton, 1936. Story of
Spanish California after the American conquest.

Paul, Charlotte. The Cup of Strength. Random, 1958.
Logging operations and life in the lumber camps of the
Northwest in the 1890's.

--- Gold Mountain. Random, 1953. Story of hop ranching,
teaching in a small town, and the effects of smallpox
on the Indians; set in a small farming community near
Seattle in the late 1800's.

Peattie, Donald Culross. Forward the Nation. Putnam,
1942. The Lewis and Clark expedition, 1805.

Peeples, Samuel Anthony. The Dream Ends in Fury. Harper, 1949. Based on the life of Joaquin Murrietta,
Mexican bandit in California in gold rush days.

Pendexter, Hugh. Old Misery. Bobbs, 1924. California
in 1853 with its mining camps, gambling houses, robber bands, and hostile Indians.

Pettibone, Anita. Johnny Painter. Farrar, 1944. Story
of the settling of the Washington Territory in the years
after the Civil War.

Ripley, Clements. Gold Is Where You Find It. Appleton,
1936. California in the 1870's during the second gold

boom. Conflict between miners and ranchers.

Roark, Garland. Rainbow in the Royals. Doubleday, 1950.
Story of a race in 1850 from Boston around the Horn
to San Francisco.

Ross, Lillian. The Stranger. Morrow, 1942. Pioneering
in the Big Sur country of California in the 1870's.

Scott, Reva. Samuel Brannan and the Golden Fleece. Macmillan, 1944. Fictional biography of the Mormon
leader, Samuel Brannan, who first reported California's
gold discovery to the world.

Shaftel, George. Golden Shore. Coward, 1943. Rivalry
between the United States, Russia, and Mexico over
the colonizing of California in the 1840's.

Small, Sidney. The Splendid Californians. Bobbs, 1928.
California in the early 19th century; details of the life
of Spanish rancheros in a new country.

Spearman, Frank. Carmen of the Rancho. Doubleday,
1937. Romance of Spanish California; a Texas scout
rescues the daughter of a Spanish don from the Indians.

Sperry, Armstrong. No Brighter Glory. Macmillan, 1942.
John Jacob Astor's fur trading expedition into the
Northwest, 1810.

Steinbeck, John. East of Eden. Viking, 1952. Chronicle
of a family who moves from Connecticut to California.
Details of country and small town life; Civil War to
World War I.

Stewart, George Rippey. East of the Giants. Holt, 1938.
Chronicle of the development of California from 1837

to 1861. Indian fighting, the American conquest, the gold rush, the rise of San Francisco and the beginnings of big business.

Stone, Irving. Immortal Wife. Doubleday, 1944. Fictional biography of Jessie Benton Fremont, wife of John Fremont, covering his part in the conquest and development of California, politics in Washington, and action in the Western campaigns in the Civil War.

Stong, Philip. The Adventure of "Horse" Barnsby. Doubleday, 1956. Romanticized story of a teen-ager's adventures in the California gold fields in the 1850's.

--- Forty Pounds of Gold. Doubleday, 1951. Panorama of frontier life from Iowa to California during the gold rush, by way of St. Louis, New Orleans, the Isthmus of Panama, and the sea voyage to San Francisco.

Teilhet, Darwin. The Road to Glory. Funk and Wagnall, 1956. Story of the Spanish missions in California in 1783; and of the work of Father Junipero Serra among the Indians; set in and near San Jose.

Terrell, John. Plume Rouge. Viking, 1942. Trek of a fur trading expedition from St. Louis to the Pacific Northwest.

Van Every, Dale. The Shining Mountains. Messner, 1948. Scout for Lewis and Clark crosses the Rockies and is captured by the Indians.

Wetherell, June. The Glorious Three. Dutton, 1951. Pioneering in the Puget Sound region at the time of the boundary dispute between England and the United States.

White, Helen. Dust on the King's Highway. Macmillan,
    1947. Story of early Spanish missionaries in Mexico
    and California in 1771.

White, Stewart Edward. Folded Hills, Doubleday, 1934.
    Continues the history of California through the Amer-
    ican conquest.

--- Long Rifle. Doubleday, 1932. Exploring in the Rock-
    ies in the 1820's. First in author's second series on
    California history.

--- Ranchero. Doubleday, 1933. Hero of "The Long Ri-
    fle" crosses the Sierras to Southern California.

--- Rose Dawn. Doubleday, 1920. Story of California's
    development during the land boom of the 1880's.

--- Stampede. Doubleday, 1942. Conflict between land-
    owners and squatters after California became a state
    in 1850.

--- Wild Geese Calling. Doubleday, 1940. Lumbering in
    the Pacific Northwest in 1895; scenes in Seattle and
    Alaska.

Young, Gordon. Days of '49. Doran, 1925. Graphic pic-
    ture of the color and excitement of the California gold
    rush.


The Plains States and the Far West

    The area west of the Mississippi River, consisting of
the present states of Kansas, Nebraska, North and South Dakota, Colorado, Utah, Nevada, Wyoming, Montana, and I-
daho were relatively late in being settled, but once started
the process was fairly rapid. In the short space of fifty

years was repeated the process of hunting and trapping, settling on new land, fighting the Indians and the hostile environment, and building a community where none had existed
before. Themes which have appealed to historical novelists
in this region are the pressing conflict with the Indians,
life on the Oregon Trail, the daily life and hardships of the
farmer-settlers of the plains, the mining boom and development of the mountain states, the migration and settling of
the Mormons, homesteading and settling of the Indian lands,
and the Pony Express and the extension of telegraph and
railroad lines into the West.

Aldrich, Bess Streeter. A Lantern In Her Hand. Appleton,
    1928. Trek of a pioneer family from Iowa to Nebras-
    ka.

---  Lieutenant's Lady. Appleton, 1942. Omaha, Nebraska
    just after the Civil War.

---  Spring Came On Forever. Appleton, 1935. Chronicle
    of pioneering on the Nebraska prairie from 1866 to the
    Depression in 1933.

---  A White Bird Flying. Appleton, 1931. Second and
    third generation of a pioneer family in Nebraska.
    Sequel to "Lantern In Her Hand."

Allen, Henry. No Survivors. Random, 1950. Background
    of General Custer's campaign against the Sioux in the
    1870's, sympathetic toward the Indians; white man
    adopted by Chief Crazy Horse rejoins Custer at the
    Battle of Little Big Horn.

Aydelotte, Dora. Across the Prairie. Appleton, 1941.
    Story of frontier settlers in Kansas in the 1890's.

Babson, Naomi. I Am Lidian. Harcourt, 1951. Theatrical
     troupe, heading west from Massachusetts in 1856 set-
     tle down in Montana two years later.

Bean, Amelia. The Fancher Train. Doubleday, 1958.
     Based on the massacre of a California-bound wagon
     train at Mountain Meadows,Utah by Mormon Danites and
     Indians in 1857.

Binns, Archie. The Land Is Bright. Scribner, 1939. Ad-
     ventures along the Oregon Trail in the 1850's.

Birney, Hoffman. The Dice of God. Holt, 1956. Fictional
     biography of General Custer and events leading up to
     the Battle of Little Big Horn.

---    Grim Journey. Minton, 1934. Story of the ill-fated
     trek of the Donner party on the way to California in
     1846.

Blake, Forrester. Wilderness Passage. Random, 1953.
     Pioneering, hunting, and trapping in the Utah Terri-
     tory and along the Oregon Trail. Conflict between
     whites and Indians, and between the Mormons and the
     United States government.

Bojer, Johan. The Emigrants. Appleton, 1925. Story of
     the Norwegian colony who settled the Red River valley
     of North Dakota, and their fight with drought, frost,
     poverty, and isolation.

Borland, Hal. The Seventh Winter. Lippincott, 1959.
     Authentic picture of cattle ranching in Colorado in the
     1870's.

Breneman, Mary Worthy. The Land They Possessed. Mac-
     millan, 1956. Story of farm and small town life in

the Dakota Territory during the late 1800's.

Brink, Carol. Buffalo Coat. Macmillan, 1944. Story of
small town life in Opportunity, Idaho, in the 1890's.

Burgess, Jackson. Pillar of Cloud. Putnam, 1957. Story
of an expedition of six men from Kansas to the Rockies
to break a new trail to the West in 1858.

Cather, Willa. My Antonia. Houghton, 1918. Life on the
Nebraska prairie.

--- O Pioneers! Houghton, 1913. Pioneer farming on the
Nebraska prairie in the 1800's.

Chapman, Arthur. John Crews. Houghton, 1926. Story of
life on the frontier around old Fort Laramie, Wyoming
involving a rescue from a group of Mormon Danites,
fights with the Indians, and Indian ceremonial life and
customs.

Clark, Walter Van Tilburg, The Ox-bow Incident. Random,
1940. A frontier Nevada town in 1885 is the scene of
the lynching of three men accused of murder and cattle
rustling.

Cooper, Courtney Ryley. The Golden Bubble. Little, 1928.
Discovery of gold in the Pike's Peak region in 1859,
organization of a People's Court in Denver, and life
in the lawless frontier towns.

--- The Last Frontier. Little, 1923. Opening of the Kansas Indian lands after the Civil War. Buffalo Bill,
General Custer and others appear.

--- The Pioneers. Little, 1938. Kit Carson and the Oregon Trail; 1842.

Corcoran, William. Golden Horizons. Macrae, 1937.
Traces the agricultural development of Kansas from
frontier days to the introduction of winter wheat.

Cunningham, John. Warhorse. Macmillan, 1956. Story of
ranch life in Montana in 1882.

Cushman, Dan. The Silver Mountain. Appleton, 1957.
Story of a man's rise to wealth and power by way of
the mining industry in Montana in the 1880's and 1890's.

Davis, Clyde Brion. Nebraska Coast. Farrar, 1939. Journey to Nebraska from the Erie Canal in 1861.

Davis, Harold Lenoir. Beulah Land. Morrow, 1949. Westward journey of a small group from North Carolina in
1851. Their journey carries them into the Southwest,
to Kansas, and on to Oregon.

--- Winds of Morning. Morrow, 1952. An old timer tells
the story of his early life as a settler in the American
Northwest, looking back from the 1920's.

Downing, J. Hyatt. Hope of Living. Putnam, 1939. Tribu-
lations of homesteading in the Dakotas.

Drago, Harry Sinclair. Boss of the Plains. Morrow, 1940.
Opening of the West, 1840's to 1860's; Mormons, General Fremont, and the Pony Express.

--- Montana Road. Morrow, 1935. Early days in the
opening of the Dakota Territory; General Custer's campaigns against the Indians and the Battle of the Little
Big Horn.

--- Singing Lariat. Morrow, 1939. Life in Nebraska just
before and after admission of the Territory to statehood in 1867. Deals with problem of whiskey runners

to the Indians, and the conflicts over statehood.

Ertz, Susan. The Proselyte. Appleton, 1933. Story of
the hardships endured by Brigham Young's Mormon
colony in Utah.

Evarts, Hal. The Shaggy Legion. Little, 1930. Story of
the passing of the buffalo; Generals Sheridan and Custer, Wild Bill Hickok, and Buffalo Bill appear.

Fast, Howard. The Last Frontier. Duell, 1941. Flight
of 300 Cheyennes from Oklahoma to Montana in 1878;
picture of the hardships of the Indians' life on the reservation.

Fish, Rachel Ann. The Running Iron. Coward, 1957. Story
of frontier life in Wyoming in the years after the Civil
War.

Fisher, Vardis. Children of God. Harper, 1939. An account of the background of the Mormon movement,
persecution in Illinois and Missouri, and the heroic
migration to Utah and the founding of an empire in the
desert; Joseph Smith and Brigham Young are major
characters.

--- City of Illusion. Harper, 1941. The Comstock Lode
gold boom; picture of life in Virginia City, Nevada in
1859.

--- The Mothers. Vanguard, 1943. Story of the Donner
party trapped in the Sierras in 1846.

Foreman, Leonard. The Renegade. Dutton, 1942. A white
man adopted by the Sioux Indians faces a decision at
the Battle of the Little Big Horn.

Frazee, Steve. Shining Mountains. Rinehart, 1951. Story

of a mixed group of Civil War veterans thrown together
in a gold rush at the close of the war; picture of life
in a mining boom-town.

Furnas, Marthedith. The Far Country. Harper, 1947. Follows a group on the long journey from Kentucky to
California in 1845.

Gardiner, Dorothy. Golden Lady. Doubleday, 1936. Gold
mining in a Colorado town from the 1880's to the Depression.

--- The Great Betrayal. Doubleday, 1949. Based on the
treacherous Sand Creek Massacre of Chief Black Ket-
tle's Cheyenne tribe near Fort Lyon, Colorado Territory in 1864 under the leadership of Col. Chivington.

--- Snow-Water. Doubleday, 1939. Saga of a small Colorado town and its founder from 1868 to 1934; pictures
the irrigation projects necessary for life on the plains,
and the growth of a town from prairie land to city.

Grey, Zane. Riders of the Purple Sage. Harper, 1913.
Story of Mormon vengeance in Southwestern Utah in
1871.

--- The U.P. Trail. Harper, 1918. The building of the
Union Pacific Railroad in the 1860's.

--- Western Union. Harper, 1939. Romance of the West
and the construction of the first telegraph lines across
the plains.

Guthrie, A. B. The Big Sky. Sloane, 1947. Fur trapping
in the Upper Mississippi River country in the 1830's.

--- These Thousand Hills. Houghton, 1956. Story of cattle ranching in Montana in the 1880's. Follows "The

Way West" (below).

--- The Way West. Sloane, 1949. Follows a wagon train from Independence, Missouri through the wilderness to Oregon on the Oregon Trail in the 1840's. Follows "The Big Sky" (above).

Haldeman-Julius, Emanuel. Dust. Brentano, 1921. A story of pioneer life in Kansas.

Hargreaves, Sheba. Heroine of the Prairies. Harper, 1930. Picture of life along the Oregon Trail in 1848.

Harris, Margaret and John Harris. Medicine Whip. Morrow, 1953. Wyoming in post Civil War days; wagon trains out of Fort Laramie, and battles with the Indians.

Haycox, Ernest. Bugles in the Afternoon. Little, 1944. The Dakota frontier and Indian-white relations preceding the campaigns of Custer against the Sioux in the 1870's.

--- Trouble Shooter. Doubleday, 1937. Construction of the Union Pacific Railroad out of Cheyenne, Wyoming in the spring of 1868.

Hough, Emerson. The Covered Wagon. Appleton, 1922. Wagon train from Missouri to Oregon along the Oregon Trail in 1848.

Hueston, Ethel. Calamity Jane of Deadwood Gulch. Bobbs, 1937. Story of early days in Deadwood, South Dakota in the 1870's; based on the life of Martha Jane Burke (Calamity Jane).

--- The Man of the Storm. Bobbs, 1936. Story of John Colter, member of the Lewis and Clark expedition, who discovered Yellowstone; scenes in old St. Louis under Spanish, French, and American flags.

Kjelgaard, Jim. The Lost Wagon. Dodd, 1955. A lone family with six children make their way along the Oregon Trail from Missouri to Oregon.

Laird, Charlton. West of the River. Little, 1953. Story of the fur trade in a town on the Upper Mississippi in the late 1830's.

Lane, Rose Wilder. Free Land. Longmans, 1938. Homesteading in South Dakota in the 1880's.

--- Let the Hurricane Roar. Longmans, 1933. Story of the pioneering days on the North Dakota prairie.

Lathrop, West. Keep the Wagons Moving. Random, 1949. Two young boys join a wagon train on the Oregon Trail; pictures life of the Indians and of the adventurous pioneers.

Lockwood, Sarah. Elbow of the Snake. Doubleday, 1958. Story of homesteading in the Snake River valley of Idaho in the 1890's.

Lofts, Norah. Winter Harvest. Doubleday, 1955. California-bound group trapped by snow in the Sierras; based on the story of the Donner party.

Lott, Milton. Dance Back the Buffalo. Houghton, 1959. Based on the rise of the Ghost Dance of the Plains Indians in 1889 and the incidents leading up to the Battle of Wounded Knee in 1890.

--- The Last Hunt. Houghton, 1954. Story of a big hunt for the last of the buffalo herds in the 1880's.

Lund, Robert. The Odyssey of Thaddeus Baxter. Day,

1957. An amusing story of the adventures of a young Texan drifting in Wyoming in the 1870's.

Mabie, Mary Louise. Long Knives Walked. Bobbs, 1932. Hardships of a California-bound wagon train over the plains and the mountains.

McKeown, Martha. Mountains Ahead. Putnam, 1961. Hardships of life on an overland wagon train on the Oregon Trail from Independence, Missouri to Oregon in 1847.

Manfred, Frederick F. Conquering Horse. McDowell, 1959. Story of a Sioux boy's search for a vision for his initiation into manhood; picture of Indian life, customs, lore, and religion.

--- Lord Grizzly. McGraw, 1954. Story of frontier revenge in the Upper Missouri River country in the 1820's.

Meigs, Cornelia. Railroad West. Little, 1937. Story of the difficulties encountered in the laying of the Northern Pacific Railroad from Minnesota to Yellowstone.

Morrow, Honoré. On To Oregon. Morrow, 1926. Life on the Oregon Trail in early pioneer days as a wagon train makes its way from Missouri to Oregon.

Parkhill, Forbes. Troopers West. Farrar, 1945. Story of a Ute Indian rebellion in Wyoming in 1879; sympathetic to the Indians' grievances.

Payne, Robert. The Chieftain. Prentice, 1953. Sympathetic account of the resistence of the Nez Perce Indians under Chief Joseph and of their valiant effort to escape to Canada in 1877.

Pendexter, Hugh. Kings of the Missouri. Bobbs, 1921.

Northwest from St. Louis to the Yellowstone country
in the days of the fur trappers.

--- Harry Idaho. Bobbs, 1926. Discovery of gold in I-
daho and the activities of the "avenging angels," the
Danite sect of the Mormons; 1860's.

Prescott, John. Journey By the River. Random, 1954.
Journey of a wagon train through Missouri and Kansas
to Fort Laramie, Wyoming in 1848.

Pryor, Elinor. And Never Yield. Macmillan, 1942. Mormons in Illinois and Missouri; Joseph Smith's death.

Rolvaag, Ole. Giants in the Earth. Harper, 1927. Picture of the Norwegian immigrant as a pioneer on the
Dakota prairie.

Rush, William. Red Fox of the Kinapoo. Longmans, 1949.
Story of Chief Joseph and the Nez Perce Indians from
1872 to 1877.

Sandoz, Mari. Miss Morissa, Doctor of the Gold Trail.
McGraw, 1955. Life on the Nebraska frontier in the
1870's; historical background of a frontier settlement
in the North Platte River country as seen by a woman
doctor.

--- Son of the Gamblin' Man. Potter, 1960. Pioneer days
in Nebraska centered around the lives of a family who
go west to found a town, enduring hardships of climate,
financial difficulties, and conflicts with cattlemen and
fellow townsmen.

Schaefer, Jack. Shane. Houghton, 1949. Life on a homestead farm in Wyoming; picture of the conflict between
farmer and rancher.

Seifert, Shirley. Those Who Go Against the Current. Lippincott, 1943. Set against the background of the founding of St. Louis, the Louisiana Purchase, and the exploration of the Upper Mississippi and Missouri River
country in the early 1800's.

Sinclair, Harold. The Cavalryman. Harper, 1958. Based
on the campaign against the Sioux in 1864, follows an
army of Civil War veterans through the Dakota Bad
Lands in pursuit of the Indians. Sequel to "The
Horse Soldiers" (Civil War).

Snow, Donald. The Justicer. Rinehart, 1960. Story of a
young lawyer's defense of an Indian on trial under a
tyrannical Federal District Court judge in Kansas in
Indian Territory in 1889.

Sorensen, Virginia. The Evening and the Morning. Harcourt, 1949. Scotch-Irish immigrants move out across
the Western plains to Utah.

--- A Little Lower Than the Angels. Knopf, 1942. Story
of the Mormons in Nauvoo, Illinois.

Steele, Wilbur. Diamond Wedding. Doubleday, 1950.
Chronicle of a typical mountain man and frontier scout
in Colorado and the founding of Denver; 1835 to 1919.

Straight, Michael. Carrington. Knopf, 1960. Based on
the Fetterman Massacre in Northern Wyoming in 1866
when the Sioux ambushed and killed Col. Fetterman
and his men who were marching against the orders of
Col. Carrington; story of Carrington's life and of the
events leading up to the massacre.

Swain, Virginia. The Dollar Gold Piece. Farrar, 1942.

Background of the livestock industry in Kansas City in
the boom years, 1887 to 1888.

Taylor, Robert Lewis.  The Travels of Jamie McPheeters.
Doubleday, 1958.  Hair raising adventures are encountered by an adolescent boy and his father as they
make their way from Louisville to the California gold
fields in 1849; capture by bandits, torture by Indians,
a short stay with the Mormons, and settling on a
ranch in California.

Waters, Frank.  The Wild Earth's Nobility.  Liveright, 1935.
Settling of Colorado after the Civil War; the mining
boom; the development of Colorado Springs.

Wellman, Paul.  The Bowl of Brass.  Lippincott, 1944.
Settling of the range country of Western Kansas in
1889, and the growth of county politics and land promotion.

Wellman, Manly Wade.  Candle of the Wicked.  Putnam,
1960.  Story of a Civil War veteran and his search for
land in Kansas in 1873; action centers around a wilderness tavern on the road from Fort Scott to Independence.

Whipple, Maurine.  Giant Joshua.  Houghton, 1941. Story of
the settlement of the Dixie Mission in the desert of
Utah by a band of Mormons in the 1860's.

## The Civil War - Before and After

Among the novels dealing with the period of the Civil War are, of course, those which deal with specific battles and campaigns of the war and with the lives of military and government leaders on both sides. There is, however, a wide range of subject matter far removed from the battlefields. There are novels set against a background of the ante-bellum South, a South of manors, mammies, and mint juleps; novels of social life in the Eastern and Southern cities; stories of the abolitionist movement; stories of families, both North and South, torn between conflicting ideals and loyalties; and novels depicting the conflict between Southern sympathizers and those loyal to the Union in the struggle to influence the Western states. Blockade running and international diplomacy, spies, prison camps, and the activities of Copperheads furnish the motif for others. And there are novels dealing with the period of Reconstruction following the war. These novels are divided into the following sections: "The Old South," "Abolition," "The Civil War," and "Reconstruction."

### The Old South

Life in the South before the Civil War, as reflected in the romantic school of historical fiction, was one of great plantations, loyal slaves, and a leisurely social life. During the 1930's and 1940's, a period during which there was a stream of reappraisals of Civil War history, a more complete picture of life in the South began to emerge. As a result

111

of this revisionist trend novelists took a fresh approach to the people of the South, concerning themselves with the pioneer-like daily existence of the small farmer, and the economic struggles of the planter and his relation with the Negroes.

Bontemps, Arna. Black Thunder. Macmillan, 1936. Story of Gabriel's Insurrection in 1810, when 1,100 slaves plotted to seize Richmond.

Brown, Joe David. The Freeholder. Morrow, 1949. Follows the fortunes of a Carolina plantation overseer through immigration to Alabama and on to the time when his slavery hating sons leave to join the Union army in 1861.

Campbell, Thomas. Old Miss. Houghton, 1929. A chronicle of Virginia life from the days of the great plantations, loyal slaves, and leisurely social life to the days of poverty brought on by the war and Reconstruction.

Cather, Willa. Sapphira and the Slave Girl. Knopf, 1940. Relations of the mistress of a Virginia plantation and an intelligent slave girl; 1850's.

Gaither, Frances. Double Muscadine. Macmillan, 1949. Plantation life in Mississippi in the 1850's exposed in the trial of a young kitchen slave accused of poisoning the plantation owner's family.

---    Follow the Drinking Gourd. Macmillan, 1940. Plantation life in Georgia and Alabama; the drinking gourd is the Big Dipper which guides the Negroes on their way north on the Underground Railroad.

--- The Red Cock Crows. Macmillan, 1944. A young Northerner sympathetic to the slaves is forced to take part in suppressing a slave rebellion in Mississippi in the 1830's.

Gordon, Caroline. Penhally. Scribner, 1931. Family chronicle of plantation life from 1826 through the Civil War and on into the "new South" of this century.

Gray, Elizabeth. Jane Hope. Viking, 1934. Picture of home life in the South just before the Civil War; Chapel Hill, North Carolina.

Griswold, Francis. Sea Island Lady. Morrow, 1939. Long chronicle of a Southern family near Beaufort, South Carolina from the Civil War to the 1920's.

--- Tides of Malvern. Morrow, 1930. Chronicle showing scenes from each generation from Colonial times through World War I, set at a plantation house on the river above Charleston, South Carolina.

Henkle, Henrietta. Deep River. Harcourt, 1944. Pictures the difference between land owning aristocrats in the lowlands and the mountainneers in Georgia in 1859.

--- Fire in the Heart. Harcourt, 1948. The heroine's debut in Covent Garden is followed by her unsuccessful marriage to the slave-holding owner of a Sea Island, Georgia plantation; picture of the temper of the times in England and America in the years preceding the Civil War. Based on the life of Fanny Kemble.

Kane, Harnett T. The Gallant Mrs. Stonewall. Doubleday, 1957. Life of Anna Morrison, Southern belle who later married Stonewall Jackson.

--- Pathway to the Stars. Doubleday, 1950. Fictional biography of John McDonough, who made a fortune in New Orleans in the 1840's and left it all to his pet projects, a plan for the slaves to earn their freedom and a public school system for the children of Louisiana.

McMeekin, Clark (pseud.) Show Me a Land. Appleton. 1940. Horse racing, gypsies, tobacco raising, and politics in Virginia and Kentucky from 1816 to 1875.

--- Red Raskall. Appleton, 1943. Romance of tidewater Virginia, beginning in 1816; plantation life and horse racing; introduces some characters from "Show Me a Land" (above).

Miller, Caroline. Lamb In His Bosom. Harper, 1933. Pioneer life on a Georgia farm from 1810 through the Civil War.

Roberts, Walter. Royal Street. Bobbs, 1944. Sectionalism and conflicting ideals leading to the Civil War are indicated in the conflict between Creoles and encroaching Northern business men in New Orleans in the 1840's.

Seifert, Shirley. Proud Way. Lippincott, 1948. Natchez plantation life during the years 1843-1844; story of the courtship of Varina Howell and Jefferson Davis.

Settle, Mary Lee. Know Nothing. Viking, 1960. Story of plantation family life and politics in the twenty years before the Civil War in the area which became West Virginia; authentic picture of the South in that period.

Stevenson, Janet. The Ardent Years. Viking, 1960. Based on the life of Fanny Kemble, English actress who married a wealthy American planter; picture of Southern social life and conflicting views about slavery in the years before the war.

Warren, Lella. Foundation Stone. Knopf, 1940. Chronicle of the South from 1823 through the Civil War; pictures the migration to Alabama from worn out land in South Carolina, and the planters' economic struggles and relations with the Negroes.

Young, Stark. Heaven Trees. Scribner, 1926. Picture of lavish hospitality, genial conversation, and light hearted romance on a Mississippi plantation in the years before the Civil War.

Abolition

Novels of the Abolitionist movement develop some exciting themes; the free-soil struggle for Kansas, John Brown's raid, the Underground Railroad, and the life and times of various real and fictitious leaders in the movement.

Allis, Marguerite. Free Soil. Putnam, 1958. Continues the story of the Cincinnati Fields, one of whom marries a Southern belle, moves to Kansas Territory and becomes involved in the struggle over the slavery versus free-soil issue in the 1840's. Sequel to "The Rising Storm" (below).

--- The Rising Storm. Putnam, 1955. Operations of the Underground Railroad in Cincinnati. Fourth in the author's series on Ohio history (see Expanding Frontiers - the Middle West).

Barney, Helen Corse. Green Rose of Furley. Crown, 1953. A Quaker girl on a farm near Baltimore helps runaway slaves on the Underground Railroad.

Brown, Katharine. The Father. Day, 1928. A New England Abolitionist settles in Illinois and publishes an anti-slavery newspaper which attracts the attention of Abraham Lincoln.

Burnett, William Riley. The Dark Command. Knopf, 1938. Picture of the warfare between free-soil Kansans and Quantrill's guerrillas and the burning of Lawrence, Kansas.

Buster, Greene B. Brighter Sun. Pageant, 1954. Story of slavery on a Kentucky plantation, and of the escape to freedom with the help of the Underground Railroad.

Cannon, LeGrand. A Mighty Fortress. Farrar, 1937. Growth of the Abolitionist movement in New England; set in Boston and New Hampshire in the 1850's.

Davis, Julia. Bridle the Wind. Rinehart, 1953. Struggle of a plantation owner's wife to regain acceptance in her home after helping a slave escape to freedom in the 1840's. Followed by "Eagle on the Sun" (Expanding Frontiers - Southwest).

Dell, Floyd. Diana Stair. Farrar, 1932. Heroine takes part in the Feminist, Socialist, and Abolitionist movements; Boston in the 1840's.

Ehrlich, Leonard. God's Angry Man. Simon and Schuster, 1932. Biographical novel of the turbulent life of John Brown.

Fuller, Edmund. Star Pointed North. Harper, 1946. Fictional biography of Frederick Douglass, escaped slave who became an outstanding Negro leader in the Abolitionist movement.

Gruber, Frank. The Bushwackers. Rinehart, 1959. Story
of the aftermath of the raid and massacre of Abolitionists at Lawrence, Kansas by Quantrill's raiders in
1863.

Howard, Elizabeth. North Wind Blows Free. Morrow,
1949. Story of a Michigan girl in the days of the
Underground Railroad, and the founding of a community
in Ontario for the fugitives.

Lewis, Sinclair. The God-Seeker. Random, 1949. A
carpenter doing missionary work among the Sioux Indians later becomes a builder in St. Paul, Minnesota,
organizes a union, and fights for the rights of Negroes
to join; Minnesota in the 1840's.

Longstreth, Thomas. Two Rivers Meet In Concord. Westminster, 1946. Abolitionist sentiment in Massachusetts; 1840's-1850's. Thoreau and Emerson appear.

Lynn, Margaret. Free Soil. Macmillan, 1920. History of
the free-soil struggle in Kansas.

--- Land of Promise. Little, 1927. Settling of Kansas
and the conflict between free and slave state supporters.

Nelson, Truman. The Sin of the Prophet. Little, 1952.
The trial of an escaped slave under the Fugitive Slave
Law in Boston in 1854; introduces many notable Abolitionists of the day including Theodore Parker and Wen-
dell Phillips.

--- The Surveyor. Doubleday, 1960. Story of John Brown
and the development of the free-soil movement in Kansas in the years following the Kansas-Nebraska Act of

1854.

Niles, Blair. East By Day. Farrar, 1941. Story of the
mutiny of the crew of a slave ship captured off Long
Island in 1839. Heroine with Abolitionist sympathies
discovers her grandfather's fortune was made in the
slave trade.

Parrish, Anne. Clouded Star. Harper, 1948. Story of a
small slave boy sold away from his parents who joined
others on the journey to the North by way of the Underground Railroad under the guidance of Harriet Tubman.

Robertson, Constance. Fire Bell in the Night. Holt, 1944.
Abolition and the Underground Railroad in Syracuse,
New York in the 1850's.

Stern, Philip Van Doren. The Drums of Morning. Doubleday, 1942. Panoramic picture of the Abolitionist
movement from the 1830's to the 1860's; John Brown,
the Underground Railroad, the free-soil struggle in
Kansas, and scenes of life in Andersonville prison.

Strachey, Rachel. Marching On. Harcourt, 1923. The
Feminist and Abolitionist movements in Michigan in the
1840's and later in Kansas.

Swift, Hildegarde. Railroad to Freedom. Harcourt, 1932.
Story of Harriet Tubman, Negro slave who escaped in
Maryland about 1821 and became a leader in the Under-
ground Railroad.

Wills, Grace. Murphy's Bend. Westminster, 1946. Frontier settlement on the Susquehanna River becomes a
station on the Underground Railroad.

The Civil War

Novels dealing with military and naval engagements of the war itself range through the entire course of the war, from Fort Sumter to Appomattox, and through all phases of the conflict, from the drive down the Mississippi River to the final push against Richmond which culminated in Lee's surrender, naval warfare, and the plots to win the West over to one side or the other. No less important in the fictional literature of the period is the effect of the war on the home front. The occupation of the old plantation house by Yankee troops, conflicts in areas of neutrality, Copperhead activity in the North and in the West, the exciting life of spies on both sides, the terrible conditions in prison camps, and the lives of political and military leaders are represented in novels of the Civil War.

Allen, Henry. Journey to Shiloh. Random, 1960.
    Seven young Texans who set out in 1862 for Richmond
    are recruited into the Army of the Mississippi and see
    action under General Bragg at the Battles of Corinth
    and Shiloh.

Allen, Hervey. Action at Aquila. Farrar, 1938. Picture
    of the war in the Shenandoah Valley in 1864.

Andrews, Robert. Great Day In the Morning. Coward,
    1950. Southern conspirators working for the South in
    Colorado in the 1850's; growing bitterness between
    Northern and Southern sympathizers in the West.

Babcock, Bernie. Soul of Abe Lincoln. Lippincott, 1923.
    Story of Lincoln's influence on the lives of a Union
    soldier and his Southern fiance.

Bacheller, Irving. Father Abraham. Bobbs, 1925. Story
of conflicting ideals in the North; Lincoln does not
appear, but his influence is felt.

Basso, Hamilton. The Light Infantry Ball. Doubleday,
1959. Southern traditions and Confederate politics
seen through the experiences of a South Carolina rice
planter from his college days at Princeton, service
through the war as assistant in the Confederate cab-
inet at Richmond, and after the war when everything
is lost.

Beebe, Elswyth Thane. Yankee Stranger. Duell, 1944.
Williamsburg, Virginia in the 1860's. Sequel to
"Dawn's Early Light" (American Revolution)

Bellah, James. The Valiant Virginians. Ballantine, 1953.
Story of the Virginia cavalry in the Army of the Shenandoah under Jubal Early and of their defeat by Sheridan.

Borland, Hal. The Amulet. Lippincott, 1957. Confederate
sympathizers making their way from Denver to join
the Confederacy in 1861 become involved in the Battle
of Wilson's Creek, Missouri.

Boyd, James. Marching On. Scribner, 1927. The war as
seen by a Southern soldier on the march, in battle
against Sherman's march to the sea through Georgia,
and in a Federal prison camp. Hero is a descendant
of the characters in "Drums" (American Revolution).

Boyd, Thomas Alexander. Samuel Drummond. Scribner,
1925. Life on an Ohio farm before and after the Civil
War.

Bradford, Roark.  Kingdom Coming.  Harper, 1933.  Negro
    life on a Louisiana plantation during the war.

---  Three-Headed Angel.  Harper, 1937.  Family sketches
    of different types living in Western Tennessee during
    the war.

Brick, John.  Jubilee.  Doubleday, 1956.  Follows a regi-
    ment of New York volunteers through the campaigns
    and battles at Gettysburg, Lookout Mountain and the
    siege of Chattanooga, the capture and burning of At-
    lanta, and Sherman's march to the sea.

---  Troubled Spring.  Farrar, 1950.  A Union soldier re-
    turns to his Hudson River valley home to find it a
    growing commercial center.

Brier, Royce.  Boy In Blue.  Appleton, 1937.  The war in
    the Cumberland Valley and the Battle of Chickamauga
    in 1863 as it appeared to a Union soldier.

Bristow, Gwen.  The Handsome Road.  Crowell, 1938.
    Life in a small river town in Louisiana before, during,
    and after the war; 1859-1885.  Sequel to "Deep Sum-
    mer" (Expanding Frontiers - Southern).

Bromfield, Louis.  Wild Is the River.  Harper, 1941.
    Story of life in New Orleans during the occupation by
    Union troops under General Benjamin Butler.

Burress, John.  Bugle In the Wilderness.  Vanguard, 1958.
    Life on a farm in the Missouri wilderness during the
    Civil War.

Castor, Henry.  The Spanglers.  Doubleday, 1948.  Details
    of soldiering in the Union army and of life in Ander-
    sonville prison.

Catton, Bruce. Banners at Shenandoah. Doubleday, 1955.
Story of General Phil Sheridan's Union cavalry opera-
tions in the Shenandoah Valley; the Battles of Boonville,
Missionary Ridge, and Cedar Creek.

Chambers, Robert W. Secret Service Operator 13. Appleton, 1934. Adventures of a woman spy for the Union
who falls in love with her opponent.

--- The Whistling Cat. Appleton, 1932. Experiences of
two young Texans serving as telegraph operators in
the Union army.

Churchill, Winston. The Crisis. Macmillan, 1901. Story
peopled by carpetbaggers, abolitionists, and Southern
gentlemen, including a Confederate spy; hero is an
anti-slavery New Englander, heroine is a descendant
of a character in "Richard Carvell" (American Revolution).

Coker, Elizabeth. India Allen. Dutton, 1953. Charleston,
South Carolina during the war and Reconstruction.

Corbett, Elizabeth. Faye's Folly. Appleton, 1941. Romance of the Civil War and politics on an Illinois
farm.

Crabb, Alfred Leland. Dinner at Belmont. Bobbs, 1942.
Nashville, Tennessee before and during the war; action
takes place in and near the city under siege.

--- Home To Tennessee. Bobbs, 1952. Effort of the
Confederates, under General Hood and Nathan Bedford
Forest, to recapture Nashville.

--- Lodging At the Saint Cloud. Bobbs, 1946. Three
Southern spies elude the Yankees in Nashville in the

summer of 1862 when the Union army was occupying
the city.

--- Mockingbird Sang At Chickamauga. Bobbs, 1949. The
war around Chattanooga in 1863; Battles of Chickamauga,
Missionary Ridge, and Lookout Mountain.

--- Peace At Bowling Green. Bobbs, 1955. Picture of
life in the South and the development of Bowling Green,
Kentucky, from the early 1800's through the Civil War.

Crane, Stephen. The Red Badge of Courage. Appleton,
1895. Psychological study of a young Union soldier in
his first action at the Battle of Chancellorsville in
1863.

Deland, Margaret. The Kays. Harper, 1926. Experiences
of a conscientious objector during the Civil War.

Delmar, Viña. Beloved. Harper, 1956. Life of Judah P.
Benjamin, Confederate Secretary of State, from his
boyhood in Charleston to his death in Paris in 1884.

Devon, Louis. Aide To Glory. Crowell, 1952. Fictionized
biography of John Rawlins, Grant's aide-de-camp and
later his Secretary of War.

Dixon, Thomas. The Man In Gray. Appleton, 1921. Portrait of Robert E. Lee.

Doneghy, Dagmar. The Border; a Missouri Saga. Morrow,
1931. Picture of the ravages of war on the Missouri-
Kansas border.

Dowdey, Clifford. Bugles Blow No More. Little, 1937.
Richmond, Virginia from secession to the evacuation of
the city in the last year of the war.

--- The Proud Retreat. Doubleday, 1953. Story of the
attempt to save some of the Confederate treasury in a
wagon train in the retreat from Richmond.

--- Where My Love Sleeps. Little, 1945. Picture of the
last year of fighting in and around Petersburg and
Richmond.

Edgerton, Lucille. Pillars of Gold. Knopf, 1941. The
West in Civil War days; the gold rush in Arizona, and
secessionist activities in the Southwest.

Edmonds, Walter D. Big Barn. Little, 1930. Farm life
in the Black River valley of New York in the 1860's.

--- Cadmus Henry. Dodd, 1949. Soldier on desk detail
and scout duty for Robert E. Lee floats over enemy
lines in a balloon.

Eliot, George Fielding. Caleb Pettingill, U.S.N. Messner,
1956. Story of a Union officer commanding a ship
blockading Southern ports.

Erdman, Loula. Many a Voyage. Dodd, 1960. Biographical novel of Edmund G. Ross, as anti-slavery newspaper editor in Kansas during the free-soil movement,
service in the Civil War, as Senator from Kansas casting the deciding vote in Andrew Johnson's impeachment
trial, as promoter of western railroad expansion, and
as territorial governor of New Mexico; 1848 to 1889.

Fairbank, Janet Ayer. Bright Land. Houghton, 1932. Story
of life in Galena, Illinois, showing the effect of the
Mississippi River trade, the California gold rush, and
the Civil War on the town.

--- The Cortlands of Washington Square. Bobbs, 1922.

New York City social life in the early days of the war.

Ferrel, Elizabeth and Margaret Ferrel.  Full of Thy Riches.
M. S. Mill, 1944.  Growth of oil companies, politics,
and Confederate raids in the new state of West Virginia; John D. Rockefeller as a young man appears.

Feuille, Frank.  The Cotton Road.  Morrow, 1954.  A
crippled Southern boy and a young Englishman transport cotton by wagon train to Brownsville, Texas for
shipment to the Glasgow cotton mills.

Foote, Shelby.  Shiloh.  Dial, 1952.  Centers around the
Battle of Shiloh in the spring of 1862.

Fox, John.  Little Shepherd of Kingdom Come.  Scribner,
1903.  Kentucky mountain people before and during the
war; description of college life, the conflicting feelings
about the war in Kentucky, and Morgan's raiders.

Frederick, Harold.  The Copperhead.  1893.  Story of the
problems of an upstate New York farmer with pro-
Southern sympathies.

Garland, Hamlin.  Trail-Makers of the Middle Border. Macmillan, 1926.  Fictional biography of the author's father who met Grant as a businessman in Galena, Illinois, joined the Union army, and participated in
Grant's Vicksburg campaign.

Garth, David.  Gray Canaan.  Putnam, 1947.  Spy story
centering around the revelation of Southern war plans.

Glasgow, Alice.  Twisted Tendril.  Stokes, 1928.  Biographical novel of John Wilkes Booth.

Glasgow, Ellen.  Battle-Ground.  Doubleday, 1920.  Picture
of Virginia plantation life before secession contrasted

with the hardships imposed by war.

Gordon, Caroline.  None Shall Look Back.  Scribner, 1937.
The Western campaigns in 1862-1863; Ft. Donelson and
Chickamauga; central figure is Nathan Bedford Forest.

Grubb, Davis.  A Dream Of Kings.  Scribner, 1955.  Story
of young love in Western Virginia from 1855 to 1864.

Hart, Scott.  Eight April Days.  Coward, 1949.  Story of
the campaign of Robert E. Lee in the days preceding
the surrender at Appomattox.

Haycox, Ernest.  The Long Storm.  Little, 1946.  Fight of
the Copperheads to take Oregon out of the Union.

Heyward, Du Bose.  Peter Ashley.  Farrar, 1932. Story of
a sensitive young Southerner witnessing events leading
to secession and war in Charleston, South Carolina.

Horan, James David.  Seek Out and Destroy.  Crown, 1958.
Based on the raiding trip of the Confederate ship
"Shenandoah" in the last months of the war; describes
the hardships of the voyage and the conflicts leading to
mutiny during the trip.

Hutchens, Jane.  Timothy Larkin.  Doubleday, 1942. Story
of an adventurer who returns from the California gold
fields, settles in Missouri, and joins the Union army
as a scout; 1852 through the war.

Johnston, Mary.  Drury Randall.  Little, 1934. Study of a
Virginia gentleman from 1850 to just after the war.

---    The Long Roll.  Houghton, 1911.  Military biography
of Stonewall Jackson, vividly describing his campaigns
from the Confederate point of view.

--- Miss Delicia Allen. Little, 1933. Life on a Virginia
plantation before and during the war.

Kane, Harnett T. Bride of Fortune. Doubleday, 1948.
Story of Varina Howell Davis from the time she first
met Jefferson Davis to the time he is released from
prison after the war.

--- Lady of Arlington. Doubleday, 1953. Based on the
life of Mary Custis, wife of Robert E. Lee.

--- The Smiling Rebel. Doubleday, 1955. Story of Belle
Boyd, Confederate spy.

Kantor, MacKinlay. Andersonville. World, 1955. Story
of the Confederacy's largest prison camp at Andersonville, Georgia.

--- Arouse and Beware. Coward, 1936. Escape of two
Union prisoners from Belle Isle, Virginia prison camp.

--- Long Remember. Coward, 1945. Picture of life in
Gettysburg, Pennsylvania on the day of the great battle.

Kelland, Clarence Buddington. Arizona. Harper, 1939.
Arizona in Civil War days; gamblers and desperados,
robberies, and Indian raids.

Kelly, Eleanor. Richard Walden's Wife. Bobbs, 1950. Pioneer days in Wisconsin before and during the Civil
War; Southern wife loyal to her husband even after
his death.

Kennelly, Ardyth. The Spur. Messner, 1951. Story of
John Wilkes Booth, of his life in the theatre, and of
the forces that drove him to the assasination of Lincoln.

Keyes, Frances Parkinson. The Chess Players. Farrar, 1960. Family affairs and social life in New Orleans in the mid-1800's; centered around Paul Charles Morphy, chess expert, and the activities of the Confederate representatives in Paris during the Civil War.

Knox, Rose Bell. Grey Caps. Doubleday, 1932. Story of two children on a Southern plantation showing the attitude of the South to the war.

Kroll, Harry Harrison. The Keepers of the House. Bobbs, 1940. Conflict between two brothers on a Mississippi plantation before and during the war.

Lancaster, Bruce and Lowell Brentano. Bride of a Thousand Cedars. Stokes, 1939. Story of Southern blockade running.

Lancaster, Bruce. Night Watch. Little, 1958. Based on the Kilpatrick-Dahlgren raid to free Union prisoners in Richmond in 1863; two cavalrymen are captured, imprisoned in Libby Prison, escape and make their way to Tennessee where they participate in the Battle of Franklin.

--- No Bugles Tonight. Little, 1948. Campaigns in the Tennessee Valley from 1862 to the relief of Nashville; Union spy is among the secret Union sympathizers in the city.

--- Roll, Shenandoah. Little, 1956. Story of the Shenandoah Valley campaign of 1864 with description of General Sheridan's victories at Opequon and Cedar Creek and the Confederates' burning of Chambersburg; narrator is a newspaper reporter.

--- The Scarlet Patch. Little, 1947. Story of the Rochambeau Rifles, a New York company, in the fighting during the first year of the war.

Lincoln, Joseph Crosby. Storm Signals. Appleton, 1935. Story of Cape Cod in the early days of the war.

Longstreet, Stephen. Gettysburg, Farrar, 1961. Story of the daily life of the people of Gettysburg, Pennsylvania as the battle develops nearby.

Lytle, Andrew. The Long Night. Bobbs, 1936. Story of revenge set in Georgia and Alabama; protagonist participates in the Battle of Shiloh.

--- The Velvet Horn. McDowell, 1957. Story of complex family relationships and of a boy growing up in the Cumberland Mountains on the Tennessee wilderness frontier during and after the Civil War.

McGehee, Thomasine. Journey Proud. Macmillan, 1939. Pictures the declining fortunes of a large tobacco plantation in Virginia during the war.

McMeekin, Clark (pseud.) City of Two Flags. Appleton, 1950. Story of the conflict between Union and Confederate sympathizers in Louisville who refused to accept Kentucky's neutrality.

McNeilly, Mildred. Praise At Morning. Morrow, 1947. International diplomacy when England decides not to recognize the Confederacy and the Russians stage naval demonstrations at New York and San Francisco in 1863.

Mally, Emma Louise. The Mocking Bird Is Singing. Holt, 1944. New Orleans and Texas during the war; picture of city and frontier life.

Markey, Morris. The Band Plays Dixie. Harcourt, 1927.
Fredericksburg, Richmond, and Savannah in the last
years of the war.

Mason, Van Wyck. Blue Hurricane. Lippincott, 1954.
Naval warfare in the West in 1862; the Union drive
down the Mississippi River.

--- Our Valiant Few. Little, 1956. Story of a southern
blockade runner and a newspaperman who exposes war
profiteers, set in Charleston, South Carolina.

--- Proud New Flags. Lippincott, 1951. Story of naval
warfare; efforts of the South to build a navy, the
Baltimore riots, and the capture of New Orleans.

Medary, Marjorie. College in Crinoline. Longmans, 1937.
Story of a girl in an Iowa college during the Civil War.

Miller, Helen Topping. Christmas For Tad. Longmans,
1956. Vignette of Christmas with the Lincolns in the
White House in 1863.

--- Christmas With Robert E. Lee. Longmans, 1958.
Short novel depicting the Lee family's first Christmas
together after the war at Lexington, Virginia where
General Lee had accepted the presidency of Washington
College.

--- No Tears For Christmas. Longmans, 1954. A tale
of Christmas at a Tennessee plantation house, used by
Union troops as headquarters.

--- Sing One Song. Appleton, 1956. Story of persecution,
guerrilla raids, and divided loyalties in neutral Kentucky during the Civil War.

Minnegerode, Meade. Cordelia Chantrell. Putnam, 1926.

The effects of the war on social life in Charleston, South Carolina.

Mitchell, Margaret. Gone With The Wind. Macmillan, 1936. Panorama of the war and Reconstruction in Georgia; plantation life, hardships of war at home, Sherman's siege of Atlanta, carpetbaggers, Ku Klux Klan, and the rebuilding of business after the war.

Montgomery, James Stuart. Tall Men. Greenberg, 1927. Story of Confederate blockade running during the war.

Morrison, Gerry. Unvexed To the Sea. St. Martins, 1960. Story of the war from both sides centering around the siege and capture of Vicksburg.

Morrow, Honore. Forever Free. Morrow, 1927. Abraham Lincoln from his inauguration to the Emancipation Proclamation; 1861-1863.

--- Last Full Measure. Morrow, 1930. Picture of the last days of the war and of Lincoln's plans for Reconstruction; full treatment of John Wilkes Booth and the assassination plot.

--- With Malice Toward None. Morrow, 1928. Story of the conflict between Lincoln and Charles Sumner over Reconstruction policy during the last two years of the war.

Noble, Hollister. Woman With a Sword. Doubleday, 1948. Story of Anna Ella Carroll, newspaper woman and writer who is credited with planning the Tennessee campaign.

O'Conner, Richard. Company Q. Doubleday, 1957. Story of the men of one of the punishment battalions, com-

posed of demoted Union officers, who redeem themselves in heavy fighting; hero undertakes an undercover
spying mission into besieged Atlanta.

O'Neal, Cothburn. Untold Glory. Crown, 1957. Based on
the spy activities of Felicia Shover, who made friends
with Union officers in occupied Memphis in order to
smuggle medical supplies to the Confederacy.

Perenyi, Eleanor. The Bright Sword. Rinehart, 1955.
Picture of Richmond society and the story of General
John B. Hood's campaign in Tennessee in 1864; Bat-
tles of Franklin and Nashville.

Pulse, Charles. John Bonwell. Farrar, 1952. Ohio and
Kentucky frontier before and during the war.

Rhodes, James A. Johnny Shiloh. Bobbs, 1959. Story of
a nine year old Ohio boy, John Clem, who ran away
to join the Union army, won his nickname at the Battle of Shiloh, and after the war became a major in
the regular army.

Roberts, Walter. Brave Mardi Gras. Bobbs, 1946. After
the Battle of Bull Run a Confederate soldier returns to
ocdupied New Orleans to organize a spy ring; picture
of life under the occupation forces of General Benjamin
Butler.

Robertson, Constance. The Golden Circle. Random, 1951.
Story of the Copperhead movement in Ohio under the
leadership of Clement Vallandigham; plot to form the
Northwest Confederacy; Morgan's raids into Ohio; the
Dayton riot; and the Ohio gubernatorial race in 1863.

--- The Unterrified. Holt, 1946. Copperheads in upstate

New York; a Senator's son involved with a group spying for the South.

Robertson, Don.  By Antietam Creek.  Prentice, 1960.
   Story of the Battle of Antietam in September, 1862,
   points up the blunders of General McClellan.

\--- The Three Days.  Prentice, 1959.  Realistic story of
   the three days of the Battle of Gettysburg in June,
   1863.

Sass, Herbert R.  Look Back To Glory.  Bobbs, 1933.
   South Carolina in the days preceding the Civil War;
   story of the political events leading to the firing on
   Fort Sumter.

Schachner, Nathan.  By the Dim Lamps.  Stokes, 1941.
   Life in New Orleans and on a Louisiana plantation during the war and Reconstruction.

Scott, Evelyn.  The Wave.  Cape and Smith, 1929.  Sweeping
   picture of the whole war.

Seifert, Shirley.  Captain Grant.  Lippincott, 1946.  Ulysses
   Grant from his entrance at West Point to the beginning
   of the war; service in Mexico and California; his re-
   tirement to business in Galena, Illinois; beginning of
   his Civil War service as a Colonel of Illinois volunteers.

\--- Farewell, My General.  Lippincott, 1954.  Fictional
   account of the life of J.E.B. Stuart from his days on
   the Western frontier in 1855 to his death while defend-
   ing Richmond against Custer in 1864.

Shuster, George.  Look Away.  Macmillan, 1939.  Kentuck-
   ian moves to Wisconsin during a mining boom; be-

comes a Confederate spy during the war.

Sinclair, Harold. The Horse Soldiers. Harper, 1956.
Story of a Union cavalry mission behind Southern lines,
based on Grierson's raid. Followed by "The Cavalryman" (Expanding Frontiers - Plains States).

Singmaster, Elsie. Boy at Gettysburg, Houghton. 1924.
Story of a young boy who aids the Union cause at the
Battle of Gettysburg.

--- Loving Heart. Houghton, 1937. Story of the Underground Railroad in Gettysburg and of events moving up
to the Battle of Gettysburg.

--- Swords of Steel. Houghton, 1933. Story of Gettysburg,
Pennsylvania and the events leading up to the battle,
including John Brown's raid on Harper's Ferry.

Slaughter, Frank. In a Dark Garden. Doubleday, 1946.
Spies, counter-spies and a medical student fighting for
the Confederacy.

Smith, Chard. Artillery of Time. Scribner, 1939. Upstate New York farm and business life from the
1850's to the end of the war.

Stacton, David. The Judges of the Secret Court. Pantheon,
1961. Story of the assassination of Abraham Lincoln,
showing the effects of the assassination on the people
involved; unsympathetic portrait of John Wilkes Booth.

Stern, Philip Van Doren. The Man Who Killed Lincoln.
Random, 1939. The story of John Wilkes Booth and
his part in the assassination.

Sterne, Emma Gelders. No Surrender. Dodd, 1932. Life
on an Alabama plantation during the war.

Stevenson, Janet. Weep No More. Viking, 1957. Based on
the life of Elizabeth Van Lew, a Southern abolitionist
in Richmond, who served as a spy for the North,
helped Union soldiers escape from Libby Prison, and
evolved a master plan for the capture of Richmond.

Steward, Davenport. Sail the Dark Tide. Tupper and Love,
1954. Blockade running for the Confederacy between
British Nassau and Wilmington, Delaware.

Stover, Herbert. Copperhead Moon. Dodd, 1952. Pennsylvania soldier returning home, tangles with Copperheads.

Street, James. By Valour and Arms. Dial, 1944. Naval
warfare on the Mississippi River; with the Confederate
ironclad "Arkansas"; Natchez and Vicksburg under
Union occupation.

--- Captain Little Ax. Lippincott, 1956. Story of the
actions of a company of teen-age Confederates from
the Battle of Shiloh to Chickamauga.

--- Tap Roots. Dial, 1942. Story of the neutral Dabney
clan in Jones County, Mississippi; 1858-1865.

Stribling, T. S. The Forge. Doubleday, 1931. Alabama
before and during the Civil War and the era of Reconstruction. Followed by "The Store" (Nation Grows
Up).

Sullivan, Walter. Sojourn of a Stranger. Holt, 1957. Story
of a part-Negro plantation owner who finds bitterness
in the plantation society, but who comes to terms with
himself after service in the war.

Tate, Allen. The Fathers. Putnam, 1938. Conflicting
ideas in Virginia just across the Potomac from Wash-

ington; 1850's-1860's.

Toepfer, Ray Grant. The Scarlet Guidon. Coward, 1958.
Follows a group of Confederate soldiers from their
enlistment in the 43rd Alabama Infantry through four
years of war; action in the Shenandoah Valley campaign, and the Battles of Gettysburg, Fisher's Hill,
and Cold Harbor.

Wagner, Constance. Ask My Brother. Harper, 1959.
Civil War background in a story of a Southern aristo-
crat with a Yankee husband.

Waldman, Emerson. Beckoning Ridge. Holt, 1940. Story
of a neutral Virginia hill farmer caught between two
armies.

Warren, Robert Penn. Band of Angels. Random, 1955.
Kentucky and Louisiana plantation life before, during,
and after the Civil War.

Weaver, Ward (pseud.) Hang My Wreath. Funk and Wagnall, 1941. Campaign of Jeb Stuart in Maryland and
Virginia culminating in the Battle of Antietam.

Wheelwright, Jere. Gentlemen, Hush! Scribner, 1948.
Story of three young Southern soldiers in the war, and
of the conditions they find when they return home.

--- Gray Captain. Scribner, 1954. Story of the 2nd
Maryland Infantry of the Army of Northern Virginia in
the summer of 1864.

Whitney, Janet. Intrigue in Baltimore. Little, 1951. Political developments and the presidential election of
1860 in Baltimore and Illinois.

Whitney, Phyllis. The Quicksilver Pool. Appleton, 1955.

Story of Copperhead intrigue and rebellion on Staten
Island; 1862-1863.

--- Step to the Music. Crowell, 1953. Story of a divided
family on Staten Island during the war.

Williams, Ben Ames. A House Divided. Houghton, 1947.
Saga of an aristocratic Virginia family with conflicting
loyalties, and of the full sweep of the war. Followed
by "The Unconquered" (Reconstruction).

Willsie, Honoré McCue. Benefits Forgot. Stokes, 1917.
Story of a young army surgeon presumed dead by his
neglected mother.

Wilson, William. The Raiders. Rinehart, 1955. Story of
conflicting loyalties and the efforts to defend an Ohio
River town under threat of a Confederate raid.

Yerby, Frank. The Foxes of Harrow. Dial, 1946. Plantation life and politics in New Orleans; 1825-1865.

Young, Stark. So Red the Rose. Scribner, 1934. Plantation life near Natchez, Mississippi before and during
the war.

Zara, Louis. Rebel Run. Crown, 1951. Story of the dar-
ing theft of a railroad engine and the race to burn the
bridges south of Chattanooga by the Union spy, Andrews.


Reconstruction

No less a part of the Civil War is the aftermath of
Reconstruction which followed. With few exceptions, the
theme running through novels of this phase of history is the
disintegration of an affluent mode of life and the rebuilding
of a new South on the ashes of the old. The return of the

soldier to his ruined plantation and his struggle to rebuild, the loyalty of the ex-slaves, political and social upheaval in the South aggravated by fanatic Southerners, insensitive occupation troops, carpetbaggers, the Ku Klux Klan, and the belligerence of less intelligent Negroes are threads running through these novels.

Andrews, Annulet. Melissa Starke. Dutton, 1935. Story of impoverished life on a once-prosperous Georgia plantation after the war.

Campbell, Marie. A House With Stairs. Rinehart, 1950. Problems of adjustment faced by whites and Negroes on an Alabama plantation during Reconstruction; carpetbaggers, occupation troops, and the Ku Klux Klan enter the plot.

Cheney, Brainard. Lightwood. Houghton, 1939. Story of the farmers' struggle against a Yankee-owned corporation in post-Civil War years in Georgia.

Crabb, Alfred Leland. Supper At the Maxwell House. Bobbs, 1943. Sympathetic portrait of impoverished Southern gentry's efforts to rebuild a shattered culture; plot centers around a Southerner's determination to regain his family home; set in Nashville.

Fast, Howard. Freedom Road. Duell, 1944. Story of a freed slave who guides former slaves and poor white tenant farmers in founding a cooperative community in the face of local opposition.

Gordon, Armistead. Ommirandy. Scribner, 1917. Amusing story of a typical old Southern Negro sharing privations with her ex-master's family.

Harben, William. The Triumph. Harper, 1917. Story of
    an Abolitionist in a small Georgia town and his troubles
    with the Ku Klux Klan.

Herbst. Josephine. Pity Is Not Enough. Harcourt, 1933.
    Story of easy money and political graft in the South in
    Reconstruction days. Followed by "The Executioner
    Waits" (The Twenties).

Krey, Laura. And Tell Of Time. Houghton, 1938. Pic-
    ture of the confusing social, political, and economic
    problems faced by Southerners after the war; Ku Klux
    Klan, relations with Negro servants, rebuilding a
    prosperous plantation, and the struggle to establish
    law and order in Georgia and Texas  from 1865 to
    1888.

McMeekin, Clark (pseud.) Tyrone of Kentucky. Appleton,
    1954. Story of the conflicting attitudes and the prob-
    lems of Reconstruction in a divided Kentucky as they
    were faced by a Confederate veteran and his Alabama
    bride.

Miller, Helen Topping. After the Glory. Appleton, 1958.
    Story of the conflicts between ex-Confederates and
    Union sympathizers in Eastern Tennessee during the
    Reconstruction period.

Miller, Helen Topping and John Dewey. Rebellion Road.
    Bobbs, 1954. Search for a new way of life by a
    Confederate soldier who returns to find his family's
    plantation in ruins.

Page, Thomas Nelson. Red Rock. Scribner, 1898. Social
    life in the South during Reconstruction in the late
    1860's, including carpetbaggers and the Ku Klux Klan.

Pierce, Ovid William. On A Lonesome Porch. Doubleday,
1960. A young widow with her small son and mother-
in-law return to their North Carolina plantation in
1865 to begin a new life.

Rhodes, James A. Trial of Mary Todd Lincoln. Bobbs,
1959. Based on the sanity trials of Lincoln's wife
in 1875 and 1876.

Sims, Marian. Beyond Surrender. Lippincott, 1942. An
ex-Confederate officer sets out to rebuild his ruined
plantation with the aid of his mother and a few loyal
ex-slaves.

Slaughter, Frank. Lorena. Doubleday, 1959. A strong-
willed Southern belle manages her husbands plantation
during the war and faces the problems of Reconstruction and the Ku Klux Klan after the war.

--- The Stubborn Heart. Doubleday, 1950. A romance
centering around the plantation of a young doctor and
his wife who is a Union spy; has the usual elements of
Ku Klux Klan, scalawags, carpetbaggers, honest Union
men, and loyal Southerners.

Taylor, Robert Lewis. A Journey to Matecumbe. McGraw,
1961. Adventure-packed story of the flight of a 14
year old boy, his uncle, and a Negro servant from
Kentucky after a run in with the Ku Klux Klan; includes a stint with a quack doctor's medicine show on
a Mississippi River barge en route to New Orleans,
a harrowing experience at a Tennessee plantation, a
dangerous crossing of the Everglades with the guidance of friendly Seminole Indians, and various economic schemes in Key West; authentic picture of life

in the time and places involved.

Weekley, Robert S. The House In Ruins. Random, 1958.
Story of a guerrilla band carrying on the war in a
small Mississippi community; theme is the responsibility one bears to rebuild for the future.

Wellman, Paul. Angel With Spurs. Lippincott, 1942.
Story of General Jo Shelby and the group of Confederate volunteers whom he led to Mexico to join Maxim-
ilian rather than accept surrender at the end of the
war.

White, Leslie. Look Away, Look Away. Random, 1943.
Story of the group of Southerners who migrated to
Brazil after the war rather than stay on under Reconstruction, and of their unsuccessful efforts to pioneer on the Amazon River.

Williams, Ben Ames. The Unconquered. Houghton, 1953.
Picture of political, social, and economic strife in
New Orleans during Reconstruction, 1865 to 1874; development of the cotton-seed oil industry, and the tem-
perate attitude promoted by General James Longstreet.

Yerby, Frank. The Vixens. Dial, 1947. Story of New
Orleans plantation life and Reconstruction legislature.

The Nation Grows Up, 1877 to 1917

The last decades of the nineteenth century and the first decade of the twentieth witnessed a major alteration in the manner of life in the United States. This changing social, political, and industrial scene is reflected in the background of novels set in the period from the end of the Civil War to World War I. The development of financial and industrial empires, the era of railroad expansion in the 1870's, the organization of labor and the growth of unions, local and national politics, the Spanish-American War, social life of the wealthy classes and life in the small town at the turn of the century, and such cultural themes as the birth of the movie industry, the assimilation of emigrants, Mormon life and customs, and the great world expositions held during the period are some of the subjects of novels in this group.

Adams, Henry. Democracy. 1879. Story of Washington social life, and political corruption during the second administration of U. S. Grant.

Adams, Samuel Hopkins. Tenderloin. Random, 1959. New York City in the 1890's. A clergyman undertakes a crusade against gambling and prostitution in spite of corrupt police and politicians.

Anderson, Sherwood. Wendy McPherson's Son. Cape, 1916. Story of a Mid-Western small town boy who becomes a successful Chicago financier in the years following the Spanish-American War

Angoff, Charles. Journey to the Dawn. Yoseloff, 1951. A
  Russian family migrates to America and settles in
  Boston at the turn of the century. Followed by "In
  the Morning Light" (World War I).

Asch, Sholem. East River. Putnam, 1946. Story of conflicts between Jews and Irish-Catholics in New York's
  East Side at the turn of the century.

Atherton, Sarah. Mark's Own. Bobbs, 1941. Industrial
  history of a Pennsylvania coal mine from 1849 to
  1929, through the story of the mine owner, his de-
  scendents, laborers and labor organizers.

Aydelotte, Dora. Long Furrows. Appleton, 1935. Picture
  of country social life in the 1890's; Fourth of July
  picnics, quilting bees, revival meetings, school ex-
  ercises, and other local affairs.

--- Measure of a Man. Appleton, 1942. Business and
  social life in a small Illinois town in the 1890's;
  effects of mail order houses on small business, the
  coming of the automobile, and the depression of 1893.

Barber, Elsie. Hunt for Heaven, Macmillan, 1950. Picture of labor developments in the 1890's and an ex-
  periment in communal living on a Pennsylvania farm;
  Chicago's Haymarket Riots; Samuel Gompers.

Barnes, Margaret Ayer. Edna, His Wife. Houghton, 1935.
  Social and business life in a Chicago suburb and in
  Washington, D. C. through the Gibson Girl days and
  World War I to the Depression.

--- Within This Present. Houghton, 1933. Two decades
  in the life of a wealthy Chicago family from 1914 to

the 1930's; World War I; Depression; flashbacks show
the development of Chicago from 1840.

--- Years of Grace. Houghton, 1930. Background of
changing social life from the 1890's to 1930; setting is
Chicago.

Beebe, Elswyth Thane. Ever After. Duell, 1945. The
Spanish-American War, The Rough Riders, and the Battle of San Juan Hill, as seen by a Virginia war cor-
respondent. One of the author's Williamsburg series.

Beer, Thomas. Sandoval. Knopf, 1924. New York social
scene in the 1870's.

Bell, Thomas. Out of This Furnace. Little, 1941. The
steel industry in Homestead, Pennsylvania from 1881
to the 1930's; development of the labor movement and
the organizing of the Committee for Industrial Organization; Hungarian immigrant family.

Bellamann, Henry. King's Row. Simon and Schuster, 1940.
Life in a small Midwestern town at the turn of the
century.

Benson, Sally. Meet Me in St. Louis. Random, 1942.
Typical Midwestern family at the St. Louis Exposition,
1903-1904.

Berlin, Ellin. Lace Curtain. Doubleday, 1948. Long Island, New York, and Paris society in the first decade
of the century. Story of prejudice in the marriage of
a Protestant and an Irish-Catholic.

Bisno, Beatrice. Tomorrow's Bread. Liveright, 1938.
Story of the sweatshop conditions in the Chicago gar-
ment making industry in the 1890's; and of the effort

to organize labor.

Bjorn, Thyra Ferre.  Papa's Daughter.  Rinehart, 1958.
    Story of a Swedish immigrant's daughter's ambition
    and struggle to be a writer; set in New England in the
    early 1900's.  Sequel to "Papa's Wife."

--- Papa's Wife.  Rinehart, 1955.  Large Swedish family
    migrate to America and settle in New England where
    Papa becomes a minister.  Story of family life and
    customs.

Blanton, Margaret.  The White Unicorn.  Viking, 1961.
    Family life and the story of a girl growing up in
    Nashville at the turn of the century.

Brace, Gerald Warner.  The World of Carrick's Cove.
    Norton, 1957.  Nostalgic view of a young boy's life
    in a Maine seafaring-farming community near the turn
    of the century.

Brinig, Myron.  May Flavin.  Farrar, 1938.  Chicago,
    New York, and Hollywood from the 1890's to the
    1930's.

--- The Sisters.  Farrar, 1937.  Life in Silver Bow,
    Montana, San Francisco, and New York, as seen by
    the daughters of a small town druggist; 1904-1910.

Brink, Carol Ryrie.  Strangers in the Forest.  Macmillan
    1959.  Story of homesteading in Idaho in the early
    1900's; centers around a Forest Service agent sent to
    find out if the settlers were actually farming the land
    or selling the timber.

Bristow, Gwen.  This Side of Glory.  Crowell, 1940.  Life
    on a Louisiana plantation from about 1885 to the period

following World War I. Sequel to "The Handsome
Road" (Civil War).

Bromfield, Louis. Mrs. Parkington. Harper, 1943. Daughter of a Nevada mining-town hotel keeper marries a
rich robber baron and becomes famous on two conti-
nents.

Budd, Lillian. April Harvest. Duell, 1959. Story of the
daughter of Swedish immigrant parents in Chicago from
the early 1900's through the outbreak of World War I
as she struggles to support herself and get an education. Sequel to "Land of Strangers."

--- Land of Strangers. Lippincott, 1953. Story of the
struggles of a young Swedish couple to make a life
for themselves in their new country.

Byron, Gilbert. The Lord's Oysters. Little, 1957. Story
of a boy's life among the oyster men of Chester River
in the eastern shore region of Maryland about the turn
of the century.

Caldwell, Janet Taylor. Never Victorious, Never Defeated.
McGraw, 1954. Pictures the rise of American capi-
talism and the exploitation of labor in the one hundred
years from Jackson's administration to 1935.

--- This Side of Innocence. Scribner, 1946. Social novel
set in upstate New York, 1868-1880's.

Carroll, Gladys Hasty. A Few Foolish Ones. Macmillan,
1935. Depicts the lives of a few Maine farmers from
the 1870's to the 1930's.

--- West of the Hill. Macmillan, 1949. Village life in
Maine in the late 1800's.

Carson, Katharine. Mrs. Pennington. Putnam, 1939. Social
   picture of a small Kansas town in the 1880's.

Carson, Robert. The Magic Lantern. Holt, 1954. Growth
   of the movie industry from silent to sound movies in
   New York and Hollywood; 1907-1927.

Carter, Isabel. Shipmates. W. R. Scott, 1934. Story of
   a seafaring family in Maine in the 1870's.

Castor, Henry. The Year of the Spaniard. Doubleday,
   1950. The Spanish-American War and its impact on
   the United States; Cuba, Puerto Rico, and the Philippines.

Chevalier, Elizabeth Pickett. Drivin' Woman. Macmillan,
   1942. Life on a Kentucky plantation from the end of
   the Civil War to 1905; teaching school, development
   of tobacco growing enterprise, and the Kentucky tobacco war of 1905.


Clune, Henry W. The Big Fella. Macmillan, 1956. Story
   of machine politics in an Eastern state in the early
   1900's.

Corbett, Elizabeth. Early Summer. Appleton, 1942. Rural
   Illinois in post-Civil War days.

---  The Far Down. Appleton, 1939. Story of a large
   family living on the outskirts of a Midwestern city in
   1877.

---  Hamilton Terrace. Appleton, 1960. Story of a woman at the turn of the century cut off from the social
   life of her small Wisconsin community by her wealth.

---  The Head of Apollo. Lippincott, 1956. Light romance

set in a small Illinois town in the 1890's.

--- The Langworthy Family. Appleton, 1937. Family life
in a Midwestern city at the turn of the century.

--- Mr. and Mrs. Meigs. Appleton, 1940. Family life
in a Midwestern city of the 1880's.

--- She Was Carrie Eaton. Appleton, 1938. Recreates
the life of a small Ohio city in the 1870's. One of the
author's Mrs. Meigs series.

Corey, Paul. Three Miles Square. Bobbs, 1939. Picture
of agricultural America through the story of an Iowa
farm family; 1910-1916.

Crabb, Alfred Leland. Breakfast at the Hermitage. Bobbs,
1945. Story of the development of Nashville and the
rebuilding of the Hermitage in the period following Reconstruction.

--- Reunion at Chattanooga. Bobbs, 1950. Social and economic developments in post-Reconstruction Chattanooga;
1876-1890.

Curry, Peggy. So Far From Spring. Viking, 1956. Story
of ranch life in the cattle country of the Colorado
Rockies in the early 1900's.

Davenport, Marcia. The Valley of Decision. Scribner,
1942. Rise of the steel industry from 1873 through
the story of a Pennsylvania steel manufacturer's family.

Davis, Clyde Brion. Jeremy Bell. Rinehart, 1947. Life
in a small Illinois town, in Chicago, in an Arkansas
lumber camp, in the army, and in various other
places in 1897.

Davis, Harold Lenoir. Honey in the Horn. Harper, 1935.
Oregon homesteading in the early 1900's.

Dawson, Cleo. She Came to the Valley. Morrow, 1943.
Saga of a Texas border town in the years prior to
World War I. Small town life, droughts, and Mexican
raids.

Deasy, Mary. O'Shaughnessy's Day. Doubleday, 1957.
Story of family relationships of a corrupt Irish politi-
cian in Corioli, Ohio from the turn of the century to
1922.

Dempsey, David. All That Was Mortal. Dutton, 1957.
Novel of the social and economic struggles of a family
in a small Illinois town from 1889 to 1924; conveys
the manners and customs of the period.

Dowdey, Clifford. Sing for a Penny. Little, 1941. Unscrupulous financial dealings in Richmond in the
1880's and 1890's.

Downing, J. Hyatt. Sioux City. Putnam, 1940. Picture of
the growth of Sioux City, Iowa up to the year 1884.

Dreiser, Theodore. The Financier. Harper, 1912. Story
of the love affairs and business career of a Philadelphia financier whose enterprises lead finally to his
arrest and conviction for embezzlement in the late
1800's. Followed by "The Titan" (below).

---    Jennie Gerhardt. Harper, 1911. Pictures the mate-
rialism of American society at the turn of the century,
through the lives of two families, German and Irish
immigrants.

---    Sister Carrie. 1900. Depicts life of the lower middle classes in New York and Chicago with insights into the business world.

--- The Titan. Lane, 1914. Continues the story of Frank Cowperwood in the financial world in Chicago in the 1870's.

Ducharme, Jacques. The Delusson Family. Funk and Wagnall, 1939. Social and industrial developments around Holyoke, Massachusetts in the years after 1874.

Edmonds, Walter D. The Boyds of Black River. Dodd, 1953. Upstate New York is the setting of a story about a horse loving family who look with disdain at the coming of the horseless carriage.

Ellsberg, Edward. Mid Watch. Dodd, 1954. Story of the pre-World War I navy, based on the explosion aboard the cruiser "Manhattan" on its trial run in 1909.

Emerson, Elizabeth. The Garnered Sheaves. Longmans, 1948. Quaker farmers in Illinois at the turn of the century.

Erdman, Loula Grace. The Short Summer. Dodd, 1958. Life in a Missouri town during the summer of 1914, with church socials, the Chautauqua, band concerts, family gatherings, and a faint echo of the trouble brewing in Europe.

Eyre, Katherine Wigmore. The Chinese Box. Appleton, 1959. Life in the upper social circles in San Francisco in the 1880's.

Fairbank, Janet Ayer. The Smiths. Bobbs, 1925. Life in growing Chicago, from the early 1860's to the 1920's.

Farralla, Dana. The Madstone. Lippincott, 1958. Story of

character conflict between three children and their
stern mother during a summer vacation at a lake in
Minnesota in 1914.

Fast, Howard. The American. Duell, 1946. Sympathetic
portrait of Peter Altgeld, governor of Illinois during
the Haymarket Riots, a one-sided picture of the struggle between capital and labor in the 1890's.

Ferber, Edna. Great Son. Doubleday, 1945. Chronicle of
the Melendy clan and the growth of Seattle, Washington
from early Alaska gold rush days to 1941.

--- Saratoga Trunk. Doubleday, 1941. Background of
social and business life in New Orleans and Saratoga,
New York in the 1880's.

--- Show Boat. Doubleday, 1926. Life on a Mississippi
River showboat, in New Orleans and St. Louis in the
1870's and after.

Field, Rachel. Time Out of Mind. Macmillan, 1935. Story
of the declining fortunes of a New England ship building family with the passing of the sailing ship, the
coming of steam, and the beginning of the influx of
summer colonists.

Fischer, Marjorie. Mrs. Sherman's Summer. Lippincott,
1960. Story of events in the household of the matri-
arch of a large Jewish family on Long Island in 1911.

Ford, Elizabeth. No Hour of History. Ives Washburn,
1940. Politics, theater, fashions, songs, and books
as seen by a girl growing up in a small town in Iowa
from 1859 to World War I.

Ford, James. Hot Corn Ike. Dutton, 1923. Politics and

political bosses in New York City; 1880's-1900.

Ford, Paul Leicester. The Honorable Peter Stirling. Holt,
1894. A story of politics, based on the career of
Grover Cleveland; set in New York in the 1870's.

Gabriel, Gilbert Wolf. Brownstone Front. Century, 1924.
Social background of New York City in the 1890's.

Giles, Barbara. The Gentle Bush. Harcourt, 1947. Louisiana plantation life at the turn of the century showing
the conflicts in the transition from the old society to
new customs and economics.

Giles, Janice Holt. The Plum Thicket. Houghton, 1954.
Farm and village life in Arkansas at the turn of the
century, with religious revivals, Confederate re-
unions, and baseball.

Goertz, Arthemise. New Heaven, New Earth. McGraw,
1953. Doctor in New Orleans in 1909 faces conflict
between his loyalty to the past and his desire to progress with the times.

Hagedorn, Hermann. The Rough Riders. Harper, 1927.
The Spanish-American War and the United States in
the 1890's; emphasizes the disorder and mismanage-
ment of our entry into the war.

Hart, Alan. In the Lives of Men. Norton, 1937. Panorama
of national events and life in a logging town on Puget
Sound from 1890 to 1907. The depression of 1893;
Spanish-American War; the Alaska gold rush, and labor unrest.

Hergesheimer, Joseph. Three Black Pennys. Knopf, 1917.
The development of the steel industry in Pennsylvania

through the chronicle of a manufacturing family.

Holt, Isabella. Rampole Place. Bobbs, 1952. A period
piece of the American Middle West from 1906 to 1912.

Horan, Kenneth. A Bashful Woman. Doubleday, 1944.
Growth of the automobile industry as a background of
family life in a Michigan city; 1890's to World War II.

Howard, Elizabeth. Before the Sun Goes Down. Doubleday,
1946. Life in a small Pennsylvania town in 1880,
from the mansions to the hovels seen from the viewpoint of a tolerant, kindly doctor.

Howells, William Dean. A Hazard of New Fortunes. Dutton, 1890. Story of the exploitation of labor and the
unionization of industry set around the streetcar strike
in New York City in the late 1800's.

Idell, Albert. Bridge to Brooklyn. Holt, 1944. Picture of
the period 1877 to 1883 centering around construction
of the Brooklyn Bridge. Sequel to "Centennial Summer."

--- Centennial Summer. Holt, 1943. Political and social
issues of the period of 1876; Philadelphia family witnesses the opening of the Centennial Exposition, and
visits New York City.

--- The Great Blizzard. Holt, 1948. Brooklyn and New
York from 1884 to the "Blizzard of 1888." Some of
the same characters who appeared in "Centennial Summer."

--- Stephen Hayne. Sloane, 1951. Picture of social and
financial dealings in the Pennsylvania coal mining
region; 1870's-1880's; conflict between the native

Dutch and immigrant Irish.

James, Henry. The Bostonians. 1886. Satirical view of
Boston society in the 1870's.

Johnston, Mary. Michael Forth. Harper, 1919. Emergence
of the new economic and social order in the South at
the turn of the century.

Jones, Nard. Wheat Women. Duffield, 1933. Three generations of Oregon wheat growers, from the arrival of
the pioneers to the crash of the market in 1930.

Kapstein, Israel. Something of a Hero. Knopf, 1941. Life
in a small Midwestern industrial city in the early
1900's; bankers, bootleggers, iron workers, politicians,
and labor agitators.

Kaup, Elizabeth. Not for the Meek. Macmillan, 1941.
Rise of the Pittsburg steel industry through the story
of a Danish immigrant who rose to the top under
Andrew Carnegie.

Kelland, Clarence Buddington. Gold. Harper, 1931. High
finance and struggle for control of the railroads;
1860's to 1870's. Sequel to "Hard Money" (The Young
Nation).

--- Jealous House. Harper, 1934. Business, finance, and
politics; 1880's to World War I. Sequel to "Gold"
(above).

Kelly, Wallace. Days Are As Grass. Knopf, 1941. Depicts
the changes in the social structure of a small Kentucky
town from the late 1870's to the early 1900's.

Kennelly, Ardyth. Marry Me, Carry Me. Houghton, 1956.
Story of the nomadic life of a young couple in the West

in the early 1900's.

--- The Peaceable Kingdom. Houghton, 1949. Salt Lake
City, Utah in the 1890's and the difficulties which be-
set the Mormons after the death of Brigham Young.

--- Up Home. Houghton, 1955. Sequel to the "Peaceable
Kingdom" (above) presents further events in the lives
of a Mormon family in Salt Lake City in the 1890's.

Keyes, Frances Parkinson. Blue Camellia. Messner, 1957.
Story set in the rice growing Cajun country of Louisiana from the 1880's to the early 1900's; description
of life in New Orleans and the customs of the Cajuns.

--- Honor Bright. Messner, 1936. Story of an aristocratic Boston family from 1890 to 1925. Washington
politics and Boston and Virginia social life.

LaPiere, Richard. When the Living Strive. Harper, 1941.
Life in San Francisco's Chinatown; 1875-1929. Tong
wars, the earthquake, and Chinese and American social
customs.

Latham, Edythe. The Sounding Brass. Little, 1953. Chronicle of three generations of a powerful North Carolina
family following the Civil War.

Leonard, Jonathan. Back To Stay. Viking, 1929. Portrays
the life and spirit of an isolated New England village
in the 1870's.

Lewisohn, Ludwig. The Island Within. Harper, 1928. Saga
of a family of Polish Jews who migrate to New York
City in the 1870's; story of the son's medical education at Columbia and the cultural conflicts between his
Jewish heritage and Americanization.

Lion, Hortense. The Grass Grows Green. Houghton, 1935. Changing social scene in New York from the 1840's to 1918.

Lord, Eda. Childsplay. Simon and Schuster, 1961. Story of a girl's childhood in Evanston, Illinois at the turn of the century.

McDonald, N. C. Song of the Axe. Ballantine, 1957. Adventure tale of lumbering and smuggling of Chinese workers into the country; setting is an island in Puget Sound in the early 1900's.

McGehee, Florence. Bride of King Solomon. Macmillan, 1958. Story of a woman raising her children in the Ozarks; details of daily life covering the period from 1871 through the turn of the century.

McKay, Allis. They Came to a River. Macmillan, 1941. The development of the apple growing industry in the Columbia River region from the early 1900's through World War I.

McMeekin, Clark (pseud.) The Fairbrothers. Putnam, 1961. Family life, horse breeding and racing, in post-Civil War Kentucky; the first running of the Kentucky Derby in 1875.

--- The October Fox. Putnam, 1956. Family conflict on an estate in the Kentucky bluegrass country in the 1890's.

McSorley, Edward. Our Own Kind. Harper, 1946. Picture of life in the Irish section of Providence, Rhode Island in the early 1900's.

Mathewson, Janet. A Matter of Pride. Dodd, 1957. Ro-

mance of post-Civil War South Carolina and Connecticut
dealing with the Yankee wife of a Southerner connected
with the invention of a cotton loom.

Meeker, Arthur. Prairie Avenue. Knopf, 1949. The changing social scene in Chicago's South Side from 1885 to
1918.

Mian, Mary Lawrence. Young Men See Visions. Houghton,
1958. Social life and customs in a New England town
at the turn of the century; episodes of church bazaars,
carriage rides, and Decoration Day parades.

Morris, Ira. The Chicago Story. Doubleday, 1952. Story
of a German immigrant family in the meat packing
industry in Chicago from 1905 to the present.

Norris, Charles. Pig Iron. Dutton, 1926. Industrial and
financial world of New York; 1880's to World War I.

Norris, Frank. McTeague. Doubleday, 1899. Picture of
the depressing poverty of the laboring classes and of
the evils of the lust for money;set in California.

--- The Octopus. Doubleday, 1901. Story of the war between California wheat growers and the railroads they
depend upon to reach their markets.

--- The Pit. Doubleday, 1903. Novel of protest, dealing
with the Chicago wheat market, an attack on the fi-
nanciers' manipulations on the wheat exchange with no
regard for the welfare of the producers.

Norris, Kathleen. The Venables. Doubleday, 1941. Family
life in San Francisco before and after the great earthquake.

Nyburg, Sidney. The Gate of Ivory. Knopf, 1920. A ro-

mance with a political background, laid in Baltimore
in the 1890's.

O'Connor, Richard. Officers and Ladies. Doubleday, 1958.
Story of two brothers serving in the American occupation forces in the Philippines in the 1890's.

O'Daniel, Janet. The Cliff Hangers. Lippincott, 1961.
Story of the early motion picture industry, set in
Ithaca, New York in 1915.

Owens, William. Fever in the Earth. Putnam, 1958. Story
of the first oil well and of the oil boom towns in the
Texas Spindletop oil region in 1901.

Parmenter, Christine. A Golden Age. Crowell, 1942. Life
in a small New England town in the 1880's and 1890's.

Parrish, Anne. Perennial Bachelor. Harper, 1925. Panorama of American manners, fads, and fashions from
1860 to the 1920's.

Pound, Arthur. Once a Wilderness. Reynal, 1934. Family
life on a Michigan farm from 1890 to about 1913.

--- Second Growth. Reynal, 1935. Development of the
automobile industry, 1913-1930's, through the story of
the Michigan family of "Once a Wilderness" (above).

Quick, Herbert. The Invisible Woman. Bobbs, 1924. Politics and the rise of the railroad interests in Iowa in
the 1890's. Sequel to "The Hawkeye" (Expanding Fron-
tiers-Middle West).

Reniers, Percival. Roses from the South. Doubleday,
1959. Social life in and around the famous resorts of
the 1880's; settings in White Sulphur Springs, West
Virginia, Saratoga, and New York City.

Richter, Conrad. Always Young and Fair. Knopf, 1947.
Life in a Pennsylvania town from the Spanish-American War to World War I.

--- The Lady. Knopf, 1957. Story of rivalry between cattlemen and sheepmen in New Mexico in the early years of the twentieth century.

Ritner, Ann Katherine. Summer Brings Gifts. Lippincott, 1956. Light romance picturing small town life in Fidelia, Colorado during the summer of 1915.

Roberts, Dorothy James. Missy. Appleton, 1957. Picture of small town life at the turn of the century; story of a girl growing up in West Virginia.

Roscoe, Theodore. Only in New England. Scribner, 1959. New England atmosphere and folkways pictured in the story of a murder committed in 1911.

Ross, Zola Helen. Cassy Scandal. Bobbs, 1954. Business and social life and the growth of Seattle in the 1880's.

Rubins, Harold. Dream Merchants. Knopf, 1949. Picture of the movie industry from penny arcade to serials and sound, and the financial deals behind it.

Selby, John. Island in the Corn. Rinehart, 1941. Period novel of a Wisconsin town on the Fox River in the 1880's and 1890's. Sequel to "Elegant Journey" (Expanding Frontier-Middle West).

Seton, Anya. The Turquoise. Houghton, 1946. Pictures the social climb of the beautiful heroine from a Mexican hovel to a Fifth Avenue mansion in the 1870's.

Shellabarger, Samuel. Tolbecken. Little, 1956. Story of American life at the turn of the century in which old

traditional family values are in conflict with rising
commercialism.

Sinclair, Harold. Years of Growth. Doubleday, 1940.
Life in a small Illinois town from 1861 to 1893.

Sinclair, Upton. The Jungle. Viking, 1906. Pictures the
oppressed life of the workingman in and around the
Chicago stockyards at the turn of the century.

Smith, Betty. Maggie-Now. Harper, 1958. Story of
immigrant Irish and Germans in Brooklyn at the turn
of the century.

Smith, Chard. Ladies Day. Scribner, 1941. Social conditions in a New York manufacturing town in the 1880's-
1890's; exploitation of labor and the movement for
women's rights.

Sorensen, Virginia. Many Heavens. Harcourt, 1954. Mormon life and customs at the turn of the century.

Steele, Wilbur. Their Town. Doubleday, 1952. Business
and social development of a Colorado town from 1897
to the 1930's.

Steelman, Robert. Call of the Arctic. Coward, 1960. Adventures of a young Harvard man who joined the Arctic
expeditions of Charles Francis Hall in the years between 1860 and 1873.

Stegner, Wallace. The Preacher and the Slave. Houghton,
1950. Fictional biography of Joseph Hillstrom, song
writer and labor organizer for the Industrial Workers
of the World, 1910-1916.

Stephenson, Howard. Glass. Claude Kendall, 1933. Struggle between agriculture and industry in Ohio at the turn

of the century and the development of gas wells and
the glass industry.

Steuber, William. The Landlooker. Bobbs, 1957. Adventures of the sons of a Chicago harness maker in 1871
on a selling trip in Wisconsin; life in the small towns,
isolated farms, and lumber camps punctuated by a
forest fire and the great Chicago fire.

Stevens, James. Big Jim Turner. Doubleday, 1948. Labor
agitation and the I.W.W. in the Pacific Northwest;
1900 to 1913.

Stone, Irving. Adversary in the House. Doubleday, 1947.
Based on the life of Eugene V. Debs.

Street, James. Mingo Dabney. Dial, 1950. Member of the
Mississippi Dabney clan becomes involved in the Cu-
ban revolt; 1895. Sequel to "Tomorrow We Reap"
(below).

--- Tomorrow We Reap. Dial, 1949. Lumber industry
and political corruption in a Mississippi valley in the
1890's. Sequel to "By Valour and Arms" (Civil War).

Stribling, T. S. The Store. Doubleday, 1932. Picture
of Southern life in the 1880's. Traces the transforma-
tion of the Old South into the new. Sequel to "The
Forge" (Civil War).

Suckow, Ruth. The John Wood Case. Viking, 1959. Story
of small town life in Iowa at the turn of the century
and the effects on a high school senior when he learns
his father has been embezzling company funds.

Sugrue, Thomas. Such Is the Kingdom. Holt, 1940. Everyday life in an Irish community in a Connecticut factory

town in 1909.

Swarthout, Glendon. They Came to Cordura. Random, 1958. Story of a small band of Americans making their way to a rear base following action against Mexican revolutionists who attacked across the border in 1916.

Synon, Mary. Good Red Bricks. Little, 1941. Politics, horse racing, and prize-fighting in Chicago in the 1890's.

Taber, Gladys. Spring Harvest. Putnam, 1959. Life on the campus of a small college in Wisconsin in the spring of 1914.

Tarkington, Booth. The Magnificent Ambersons. Doubleday, 1918. Rise and decline of a typical Midwestern family in the 1870's.

Thompson, Ariadne. The Octagonal Heart. Bobbs, 1956. Nostalgic memories of a Greek-American family living in an octagonal house in St. Louis at the turn of the century.

Tippett, Thomas. Horse Shoe Bottoms. Harper, 1935. The early labor movement and the problems of Illinois mine workers in the 1870's and after.

Towne, Charles H. Good Old Yesterdays. Appleton, 1935. Picture of a Southern family growing up and finding a place in life in New York in the 1880's and 1890's.

Train, Arthur Cheney. Tassles on her Boots. Scribner, 1940. New York society and politics in the days of Boss Tweed and the Grant administration.

Turnbull, Agnes Sligh. Gown of Glory. Houghton, 1952.

Life of a minister and his family in a small Pennsylvania town at the turn of the century.

Walker, Mildred.  Light from Arcturus.  Harcourt, 1935.
Development of a girl's character built around the
Philadelphia Centennial Exposition, 1876, the Chicago
Columbian Exposition, 1893, and the Chicago World's
Fair, 1933.

--- The Quarry. Harcourt, 1947.  Life in Vermont from
just before the Civil War to the beginning of World
War I.

Warren, Lella.  Whetstone Walls.  Appleton, 1952. Struggles of a young doctor in Alabama at the turn of the
century.  Sequel to "Foundation Stone" (Old South).

Warren, Robert Penn.  Night Rider.  Houghton, 1939.
Story of the Kentucky tobacco war of 1905 and the development of the tobacco cooperatives.

Watts, Mary.  The Noon-Mark.  Macmillan, 1920.  Picture
of life in a prosaic American city in the 1880's.

Wellman, Paul.  Jubal Troop.  Doubleday, 1953. Story of
the rise and decline of an adventurer in the Southwest
and a picture of the oil industry; set in Texas, Mexico,
the Dakotas, and Oklahoma from 1886 to the 1920's.

--- The Walls of Jericho.  Lippincott, 1947.  Story of
social and political life in a small town in Kansas
from 1901 to the 1940's.

West, Jessamyn.  The Witch Diggers.  Harcourt, 1951.
Picture of life on a farm in Southern Indiana in 1899.

Wharton, Edith.  Age of Innocence.  Appleton, 1920. Study
of American manners and of New York's original 400

in the 1870's.

--- The Buccaneers. Appleton, 1938. Social life in New
York and Newport in the 1870's.

White, Leslie Turner. Log Jam. Doubleday, 1959. Story
of the days of the lumber barons of Michigan's lower
peninsula in the 1870's, and of the conflicts resulting
in the first attempts to break the monopoly and to in-
troduce new methods and machinery to the logging
operations.

White, Victor. Peter Domanig in America: Steel. Bobbs,
1954. Story of a young Austrian immigrant and the
steel industry in Pittsburg about 1919.

White, William Allen. In the Heart of a Fool. Macmillan,
1918. Pictures the growth of a Kansas town from the
1870's to World War I; story of political corruption
and conspicuous consumption following a mining boom.

Whitlock, Brand. J. Hardin & Son. Appleton, 1923. Picture of the political, social, and industrial life of a
small Ohio town in the 1880's.

Whitney, Phyllis A. Skye Cameron. Appleton, 1957.
Creole society in New Orleans in the 1880's.

--- The Trembling Hills. Appleton, 1956. Light romance
set in San Francisco at the time of the 1906 earthquake.

Williams, Ben Ames. Owen Glen. Houghton, 1950. The
development of the United Mine Workers union and the
American social and political scene from the viewpoint of a boy in a small town in the Southern Ohio
coal fields in the 1890's.

--- Splendor. Houghton, 1927. Picture of American family life and interests from 1872 to 1916 in the life of a newspaper man.

Williams, Elva. Sacramento Waltz. McGraw, 1957. A romance set in Sacramento, San Francisco, and Paris from about 1910 to the Prohibition era.

Winslow, Anne Goodwin. It Was Like This. Knopf, 1949. A love story set in Southern Mississippi after the Civil War.

--- The Springs. Knopf, 1949. Gentle story of a beautiful girl and her beaux at a resort hotel in a Southern town in the late 1800's.

Wise, Evelyn Voss. As the Pines Grow. Appleton, 1939. Story of a Minnesota farming community from about 1910 to post-World War I days.

Yerby, Frank. Pride's Castle. Dial, 1949. New York social and business rivalry in the 1870's.

--- Serpent and the Staff. Dial, 1958. Picture of medical and social life in New Orleans at the turn of the century.

Zara, Louis. Dark Rider. World, 1961. Fictional biography of Stephen Crane, journalist and author of "The Red Badge of Courage."

## World War I

World War I is the first period in which the major events took place outside the United States. In addition to novels depicting actual warfare, however, there are novels based on the experiences of civilian non-combatants, nurses, telephone operators, ambulance drivers; novels depicting life in the training camps; stories of German spy activity and of anti-German feeling in American communities; novels dealing with the effects of the war on the home front; and novels dealing with politics before and during the war.

Adams, Samuel Hopkins. Common Cause. Houghton, 1919. A newspaper man tries to promote patriotism in a Midwestern city in war time; conflicts created by large German-American population.

Allen, Hervey. It Was Like This. Farrar, 1940. Two stories describing what war was actually like in July and August, 1918.

Andrews, Mary Shipman. Her Country. Scribner, 1918. Story of a girl singer who gave her talents to the patriotic cause of singing for the Liberty Bond drives.

--- His Soul Goes Marching On. Scribner, 1922. The spirit of Theodore Roosevelt inspires a young soldier in the Rainbow Division in France.

Angoff, Charles. In the Morning Light. Yoseloff, 1952. Follows a family of Russian Jews in Boston up through World War I and after; development of the young son

in the public school system, the war years, and some
of the bad times afterward. Followed by "The Sun at
Noon" (1920's).

Anonyomous. Conscript 2989. Dodd, 1918. Amusing experiences in training camp related by a young draftee.

Babson, Naomi. Look Down From Heaven. Reynal, 1942.
New England village at the time of the war.

Bacheller, Irving. The Prodigal Village. Bobbs, 1920.
Story of the beginning of flapper society during the in-
flated days of 1917-1918.

Bailey, Temple. The Tin Soldier. Penn, 1918. Story of a
young millionaire of draft age whose promise to his
dying mother prevents his enlistment. Set in wartime
Washington.

Beebe, Elswyth Thane. Kissing Kin. Duell, 1948. Williamsburg, Virginia, London and the continent at the
time of the war. Sequel to "Light Heart" (below).

--- Light Heart. Duell, 1947. Williamsburg, New York,
and London customs and traditions at the time of the
war. In the author's Williamsburg series (see other
categories).

Binns, Archie. The Laurels Are Cut Down. Reynal, 1937.
The American army in the Siberian campaign and the
indifference of people at home in the Puget Sound area
of Washington.

Bonner, Charles. Legacy. Knopf, 1940. Family life and
war service of five brothers; 1905-1918.

Boyd, Thomas Alexander. Through the Wheat. Scribner,
1923. Describes the maturing experiences of a young

Marine in the war.

Bromfield, Louis. Green Bay Tree. Stokes, 1924. Saga
of a Midwestern city growing from farmland to industrial center at the time of the war.

Brown, Alice. Bromley Neighborhood. Macmillan, 1917.
Life in a New England village showing the effect of
the war on everyone in the community.

Caldwell, Janet Taylor. Balance Wheel. Scribner, 1951.
Story of a munitions family in a Pennsylvania town.

Campbell, W. M. Company K. Smith and Haas, 1933.
Experiences of a company from training camp to action in France and return.

Cather, Willa. One of Ours. Knopf, 1922. A frustrated
Nebraska farm boy prefers life as a soldier in France
to farm life.

Corey, Paul. The Road Returns. Bobbs, 1940. Farm life
through the difficult years of the war and after; 1917-
1923.

Dawson, William James. The War Eagle. Lane, 1918.
Story of the indifference of Americans to the war until
the sinking of the "Lusitania" brings the United States
into active involvement.

Di Donato, Pietro. Three Circles of Light. Messner,
1960. Story of family life in the Italian community of
West Hoboken, New Jersey during the war.

Dinneen, Joseph. Ward Eight. Harper, 1936. Politics in
the north end of Boston before and during the war.

Dodge, Henry Irving. The Yellow Dog. Harper, 1918.

Short tale of a plan to hand out a "yellow dog" card to complainers who undermine morale by finding fault with the war effort.

Dos Passos, John. Chosen Country. Houghton, 1951. Chicago and its suburbs in wartime.

--- 1919. Houghton, 1932. Camera-eye view of the U-nited States in 1919; catches the spirit of the period.

--- Three Soldiers. Doran, 1921. Military history of three men from training camp through the war and the disillusionment following demobilization.

Downes, Anne Miller. Heartwood. Lippincott, 1945. Love story of a mountain boy who takes a wife to his moun-tain home after serving in the war.

Downey, Fairfax. War Horse. Dodd, 1942. Story of a Texas mare attached to American artillery regiment in France.

Ellsberg, Edward. Pigboats. Dodd, 1931. Story of sub-marine and destroyer warfare in the war.

Fee, Mary Helen. Plain Americans. McClurg, 1926. Story of a provincial family at the time of World War I. After the death of her husband at the end of the war, the heroine joins a "Save-America" movement.

Fredenburgh, Theodore. Soldiers March! Harcourt, 1930. Combat experiences of a young American soldier.

Goodrich, Marcus. Delilah. Rinehart, 1941. Story of a destroyer of the U. S. battle fleet in the six months before the declaration of war.

Grey, Zane. Desert of Wheat. Harper, 1919. Story of German-inspired labor troubles with the I.W.W. in the

Washington wheat fields, life in training camp, and the horrors of the war in France.

Harrison, Henry. Saint Teresa. Houghton, 1922. Picture of anti-German feeling during the war; story of a steel manufacturer who refused to make munitions.

Hemingway, Ernest. A Farewell to Arms. Scribner, 1929. Love story of an American soldier and a Swiss nurse on the Italian front in 1917.

Heth, Edward H. Told With a Drum. Houghton, 1937. Effects of anti-German feeling in a German-American community in the Midwest.

Hodson, James. Grey Dawn--Red Night. Doubleday, 1930. Picture of army life from training camp to battlefield.

--- Return to the Wood. Morrow, 1955. Story of a veteran who returns to the battlefields of his youth and relives his wartime experiences.

Hunt, Frazier. Blown in by the Draft. Doubleday, 1918. Character sketches of life in an army camp, showing the variety of races and nationalities thrown together by the draft.

Knox, James. Sunday's Children. Houghton, 1955. Small-town parsonage life in the Shenandoah Valley before and during World War I.

Kyne, Peter B. They Also Serve. Cosmopolitan, 1927. Wartime experiences of a U. S. Army horse.

Lardner, Ring. Treat'em Rough. Bobbs, 1918. Humorous letters on life in an army training camp written by an illiterate Chicago baseball player.

Lee, Mary. It's a Great War. Houghton, 1929. War and
its effects on the individuals as seen by a New England
girl in the hospital, in a Y hut, and with the army of
occupation in Germany.

Lewis, Flannery. Brooks Too Broad for Leaping. Macmil-
lam, 1938. A young child's experiences while his father is serving in France.

Lewis, Herbert C. Spring Offensive. Viking, 1940. Re-
flections on his life in Indiana by a young soldier trapped in the no-man's land of the Maginot Line during a
German offensive.

Lutes, Della Thompson.    My Boy in Khaki.   Harper, 1918.
Emotional story of a mother whose son is in the army;
shows his life in training camp, his war wedding, and
his departure for France.

Lutz, Grace Livingston Hill.   The Search.   Lippincott, 1919.
Story of the Salvation Army in the war.

McClure, Robert E.   The Dominant Blood.   Doubleday, 1924.
Dilemma of a young German-American with conflicting
loyalties between his German heritage and love for his
new country.

--- Some Found Adventure. Doubleday, 1926. Story of
the life and love of an American soldier in France during the war.

McCutcheon, George B.   Shot with Crimson.   Dodd, 1918.
Story of German agents in the U. S. spying and sabo-
toging the war effort, aided by a New York society
woman.

McKee, Ruth.   Three Daughters.   Doubleday, 1938. Story of

the civilian role behind the front lines; nurse, telephone operator, and Red Cross representatives. Shows the waste and horror of war.

Martin, Mrs. George.  March On.  Appleton, 1921.  Presents the reaction of the South to the war.

Montague, Margaret.  Uncle Sam of Freedom Ridge.  Doubleday, 1920.  Eccentric old man leads the patriotic spirit of his small Virginia community; loses faith when the United States refuses to join the League of Nations.

Nason, Leonard.  Chevrons.  Doran, 1926.  The account of a soldier and his buddies on the front lines in France.

---  A Corporal Once.  Doubleday, 1930.  Adventures of a soldier through the ups and downs of war life.

---  Sergeant Eadie.  Doubleday, 1928.  Humorous account of a doughboy's experience in the A.E.F.

North, Sterling.  Night Outlasts the Whippoorwill.  Macmillan, 1936.  Liberty Bond crusades, propaganda, food conservation, in a small Wisconsin farming community during the war.

Odum, Howard.  Wings On My Feet.  Bobbs, 1929.  Negro's narrative of his part in the war.

Paul, Charlotte.  Hear My Heart Speak.  Messner, 1950.  Story of the rehabilitation of a shell-shocked veteran.

Putnam, Nina Wilcox and Norman Jacobsen.  Esmeralda.  Lippincott, 1918.  Amusing satire centering around a down to earth girl from California who shocks the New York social set into entering war work.

Richmond, Grace Louise. The Whistling Mother. Garden
City, 1917. Tells of the farewell visit home of a college boy who is leaving for the war.

Scanlon, William. God Have Mercy On Us. Houghton, 1929.
Story of the U. S. Marines at Belleau Wood in 1918.

Sheean, Vincent. Bird of the Wilderness. Random, 1941.
Reactions of the people of a small town in Illinois to
the war, seen by a high school boy with German-A-
merican relations.

Sherwood, Margaret Pollock. A World to Mend. Little,
1920. Observations of life in a New England village
during the war by a philosophical shoe mender.

Sinclair, Upton. World's End. Viking, 1940. Story of the
world munitions industry, the war, and the peace con-
ference as seen by the son of an American munitions
maker. First in the author's Lanny Budd series. Followed by "Between Two Worlds" (1920's).

Smith, Betty. A Tree Grows In Brooklyn. Harper, 1943.
Life of a tenement family in the Williamsburg section
of Brooklyn before and during World War I.

Stallings, Lawrence. Plumes. Harcourt, 1924. Story of
the futility of war, expressed in the life of a college
professor completely broken by his war experiences.

Streeter, Edward. Dere Mable. Stokes, 1918. Humorous
letters from a rookie to his girl friend relating incidents of life in a Southern training camp.

Tilden, Freeman. Khaki. Macmillan, 1918. Story of a
pacifist community jarred out of its complacency and
into the war effort by the death, in France, of the

rich spinster who was the town's only patriot.

Tucker, Augusta. Miss Susie Slagle's. Harper, 1939. Life
in a boarding house for medical students at Johns Hopkins at the time of the war.

Van Doren, Dorothy. Dacey Hamilton. Harper, 1942. Picture of life in New York City in 1918.

Walker, Mildred. Brewer's Big Horses. Harcourt, 1940.
Michigan girl flouts conventions by working as a news-
paperwoman and marrying a brewer's son.

Wharton, Edith. The Marne. Appleton, 1918. An American boy is shocked at the American attitude of selfish
indifference at the beginning of the war; at the second
battle of the Marne he discovers that other Americans
love France as he does.

--- Son at the Front. Scribner, 1923. Novel of America's participation in the war showing the feeling of
neutrality and isolationism felt by some.

Wharton, James. Squad. Coward, 1928. Story of trench
warfare experienced by a variety of American youths
thrown together by the draft.

Wise, Evelyn. As the Pines Grow. Appleton, 1939. Farm
life in Minnesota; the bitterness of anti-German feeling,
and its conflict with pacifist feeling.

The Nineteen-Twenties

The United States during the decade of the Twenties
was characterized by an extravagance, a restlessness, and
a lack of purpose which resulted in dramatic excesses, from
the frantic boom in Florida real estate to the witch hunting
of the "red" scare. Several main themes predominate in the
novels dealing with this period: the after-effects of World
War I; prohibition and gangsterism; further industrial expansion and the labor movement; mass hysteria and the red
scare; life in the jazz age; and prosperity, speculation, and
the market crash of 1929.

Abbe, George. The Winter House. Doubleday, 1957. Son
    of a small town minister rebels at a society based on
    money and social position and turns to Socialism dur-
    ing his college days.

Adamic, Louis. Grandsons. Harper, 1935. Cross-section
    of American life in the Twenties; story centers around
    a neurotic war veteran, an Al Capone henchman, and
    a labor organizer.

Adams, Samuel Hopkins. Revelry. Boni and Liveright,
    1926. Social and political life in Washington based on
    the scandals during the Harding administration.

---  Siege. Boni and Liveright, 1924. Story of the strug-
    gles of the labor unions in conflict with benevolent
    paternalism.

Anderson, Sherwood. Dark Laughter. Boni and Liveright,
    1925. Story of a newspaper man dissatisfied with the
    undemanding society of his day, who leaves his job
    and wife to go drifting.

--- Kit Brandon, a Portrait. Scribner, 1936. Depicts
    the confusion of values in American life in the Twen-
    ties; factory working conditions, and bootlegging.

Angoff, Charles. Between Day and Dark. Yoseloff, 1959.
    Continues the story of family life and customs of a
    Russian Jewish family in Boston during the 1920's.
    Sequel to "Sun at Noon" (below).

--- The Sun at Noon. Yoseloff, 1955. Story of the life
    and customs of a family of Russian Jews in Boston;
    1919-1923. Sequel to "In the Morning Light" (World War
    I).

Arnold, Oren. The Golden Chair. Elsevier, 1954. Texas
    family life in the Twenties seen through the experiences
    of two children; centers around the family grocery
    store.

Atherton, Gertrude. Black Oxen. Boni and Liveright, 1923.
    Story of life in the sophisticated social and literary
    circles of New York City of 1922.

Bacheller, Irving. The Scudders. Macmillan, 1923. Con-
    temporary novel which pictures the insecurity of family
    life of the period.

--- Uncle Peel. Stokes, 1933. Story of the financial
    boom and of its consequences; Florida real estate
    boom.

Bailey, Temple. Enchanted Ground. Penn, 1933. Story of

Florida after the collapse of the land boom.

Banning, Margaret Culkin. Spellbinders. Doran, 1922.
Story of the movement for woman's suffrage in a Midwestern city.

Beals, Carleton. Black River. Lippincott, 1934. Story of
American oil companies in Mexico; closes with the
scandal of Teapot Dome.

Bellow, Saul. Adventures of Augie March. Viking, 1953.
Picture of the lower level of American society of the
Twenties; set in Chicago.

Bethea, Jack. Bed Rock. Houghton, 1924. Realistic story
of coal mining in Alabama with conflict arising from
bootlegging and sabotage.

Blassingame, Wyatt. The Golden Geyser. Doubleday, 1961.
Story of the Florida land boom in the early 1920's,
and of its consequences for a young couple getting
started with a plant nursery.

Block, Libbie. Wild Calendar. Knopf, 1946. Story of disillusionment and unrest in Denver in the late Twenties.

Boyd, Thomas Alexander. In Time of Peace. Minton,
1935. Account of American life in the Twenties
through the story of a veteran facing up to the economic system. Sequel to "Through the Wheat" (World
War I).

Brace, Ernest. Commencement. Harper, 1924. Picture of
the problems and conflicts facing young people emer-
ging from college to face life in the jazz age.

Bradbury, Ray. Dandelion Wine. Doubleday, 1957. One
summer in the life of a 12-year old boy in a small

town in Illinois in 1928.

Brown, Fredric. The Office. Dutton, 1958. Story of a
shy office boy and of the people around him in Cin-
cinati in the 1920's.

Burgan, John. The Long Discovery. Farrar, 1950. Story
of the change, from iron-ruled company towns to the
union strength of the workers; set in the Pennsylvania
coal fields.

Burnett, William Riley. Little Ceasar. Dial, 1929. Story
of the rise and fall of a Chicago gangster, based on
the life of Al Capone and other gangsters of the Prohibition era.

Burt, Maxwell Struthers. The Delectable Mountains.
Scribner, 1927. Picture of American life and manners of the day; set in Wyoming.

Carlisle, Helen Grace. Merry, Merry Maidens. Harcourt,
1937. The story of the life of six girls as they grow
up during the post-war Twenties.

Caspary, Vera. Evvie. Harper, 1960. Story of the life of
a murdered divorcee during the high-living days of the
1920's in Chicago.

Colby, Nathalie Sedgwick. Black Stream. Harcourt, 1927.
New York society life in a novel of manners, showing
the selfishness, greed, and meaningless activity of the
period.

Cooley, Leland Frederick. The Run for Home. Doubleday,
1958. Story of the squalid conditions prevailing in the
U. S. Merchant Marine Service during the Twenties.

Corey, Paul. County Seat. Bobbs, 1941. Bootlegging;

violent stock market upsets; farm foreclosures; picture
of everyday life in an Iowa farming community.

Cowen, William. They Gave Him a Gun. Smith and Haas,
1936. Story of a confused young war veteran who
turns to crime; an indictment of post-war American
society.

Cunningham, Sara and William. Danny. Crown, 1953.
Adventures of a young cub reporter in a small Oklahoma town.

Curran, Henry. Van Tassel and Big Bill. Scribner, 1923.
Humorous story of New York ward politics.

Cushman, Dan. Goodbye, Old Dry. Doubleday, 1959. A
quack doctor tries to bolster the economy of a village
in Montana in the 1920's.

Davis, Elmer. White Pants Willie. Bobbs, 1932. Story of
the Florida boom and Chicago; 1923-24.

Davis, Wesley Ford. The Time of the Panther. Harper,
1958. Story of a boy growing up during the summer
he was 14 years old; set in a Florida lumber camp in
the 1920's.

De Capite, Raymond. The Coming of Fabrizze. McKay,
1960. Happy story of life in the Italian colony of
Cleveland, Ohio in the 1920's; the stock market crash
effects, but does not depress the characters.

Doner, Mary Frances. The Glass Mountain. Doubleday,
1942. Picture of social and cultural life in the Great
Lakes region; influence of the Chautauqua, and shipping on the Great Lakes.

Dos Passos, John. Adventures of a Young Man. Houghton,

1939. Social and economic problems of American
society met by a young man growing up in the Twenties
until his death in the Spanish Civil War. Hero is
sympathetic to Communist ideals.

--- The Big Money. Houghton, 1936. Picture of American life in the frenzied boom days from 1919 to 1929.

--- The 42nd Parallel. Houghton, 1930. Pictures the U-
nited States during the period of the Twenties.

--- Manhattan Transfer. Harper, 1925. View of various
types of life in New York City.

Douglas, Marjory. Road to the Sun. Rinehart, 1952. Story
of South Florida and the Everglades in the days when
Miami was growing.

Downes, Anne Miller. The Angels Fell. Stokes, 1941.
Greenwich Village and Westchester County from the
end of the war through the Twenties.

--- Kate Cavanaugh. Lippincott, 1958. Story of a shaky
marriage which reflects the spirit of the restless
Twenties.

--- Until the Shearing. Stokes, 1940. Story of the growing up of a sensitive boy in upstate New York.

Dreiser, Theodore. An American Tragedy. Boni and Liveright, 1925. Graphic picture of American society in
the Twenties.

Dudley, Frank. King Cobra. Carrick and Evans, 1940.
The rise of a national terrorist organization in the
Twenties.

Eastman, Max. Venture. Boni, 1927. Story of a young

man, expelled from college, who lives it up in New
York, until he becomes interested in the labor movement.

Fairbank, Janet Ayer. Rich Man, Poor Man. Houghton,
1936. Picture of the American political and social
scene from 1912 to 1929; Theodore Roosevelt and the
reform movement; women's suffrage; prohibition; the
stock market boom; and the financial crash.

Farrell, James T. Father and Son. Vanguard, 1940.
Story of Danny O'Neill growing up from the seventh
grade through high school; Chicago setting.

--- Judgment Day. Vanguard, 1935. Follows the career
of Studs Lonigan growing up in Chicago.

--- My Days of Anger. Vanguard, 1943. Follows Danny
O'Neill through his college years in the middle Twenties.

Fitch, Albert. None So Blind. Macmillan, 1924. Story of
college life set in Harvard and Boston; shows effect of
democratic ideas of the day clashing with tradition.

Fitzgerald, F. Scott. The Beautiful and Damned. Scribner,
1922. Story of a rich playboy and of the downward
spiral of his marriage during the wild excesses of the
jazz age.

--- The Great Gatsby. Scribner, 1925. Picture of the
jazz-age society on Long Island in the years after
World War I.

Fleming, Berry. To the Market Place. Harcourt, 1938.
Picture of New York social and economic life in the
Twenties.

Flint, Margaret. Back O' the Mountain. Dodd, 1940. Story
of Maine life in the Twenties.

Gann, Ernest. Blaze of Noon. Holt, 1946. Story of aviation in the Twenties when barnstorming pilots started
carrying the U. S. Mail.

Halper, Albert. The Foundry. Viking, 1934. Chicago
industrial scene, 1928-29; conflict between owners,
bosses, and laborers.

Harris, Corra May. Flapper Anne. Houghton, 1926. Story
of a typical flapper in the South in the early 1920's.

Herbst, Josephine. The Executioner Waits. Harcourt,
1934. Story of a middle class family caught in the
changing times, victims of the economic process;
1919-1929.

Hobart, Alice Tisdale. The Cleft Rock. Bobbs, 1948. Picture of power monopolies and irrigation projects in a
California valley in the Twenties.

Hull, Helen Rose. The Hawk's Flight. Coward, 1946.
Family life in Connecticut in the Twenties.

Irwin, Inez Haynes. P.D.F.R. Harper, 1928. Sympathetic
view of the self-sufficient life of rich sophisticated
youth in New York City.

Jackson, Margaret. First Fiddle. Bobbs, 1932. Conflict
between a war veteran and his career wife.

Keene, Day and Dwight Vincent. Chautauqua. Putnam,
1960. Story of the events which occured in an Iowa
town in the summer of 1921 during the visit of the
Chautauqua.

Kelland, Clarence Buddington. Contraband. Harper, 1923.
A girl newspaper editor exposes the murderers and
bootleggers in control of her town.

Kelleam, Joseph. Blackjack. Sloane, 1948. Story of a
decaying Oklahoma town brought back to life by the
discovery of oil.

Kerkbride, Ronald. Winds, Blow Gently. Fell, 1945.
Family life on a run down plantation in South Carolina; conflict with Southern conservatism on the issues
of fair wages and education for Negroes, and diver-
sified crops; activities of the Ku Klux Klan.

Kerr, Sophie. Miss J. Looks On. Farrar, 1935. Picture
of a wealthy family hit by the financial crash of 1929.

Keyes, Frances Parkinson. Victorine. Messner, 1958.
Mystery plot set in the rice growing country of Louisiana in the mid-1920's, showing the manners and customs of the time.

Levin, Meyer. Complusion. Simon and Schuster, 1956.
Fictionized account of the Leopold-Loeb murder case
in Chicago in 1925.

--- Old Bunch. Viking, 1937. Reunion in Chicago during
the World's Fair in 1934; characters review events in
their lives since 1921.

Lewis, Sinclair. Arrowsmith. Harcourt, 1925. Picture
of medical education and practice; story of a doctor
through medical school and general practice as a
country doctor to his conflicts with politics in public
health work.

--- Babbitt. Harcourt, 1922. Picture of American mid-

dle-class life, through the story of a conservative
Republican real estate agent.

--- Elmer Gantry. Harcourt, 1927. An attack on the
hypocrisy of the times centering around the story of
the sensational rise of an evangelist.

Longstreet, Stephen. The Crime. Simon and Schuster,
1959. Story of the murder of a minister and his mistress, based on the Halls-Mills murder case in New
Jersey in 1922.

McGibeny, Donald. Slag. Bobbs, 1922. Story of conflict
between management and labor in a steel mill; characters are an arrogant capitalist, a labor agitator, and
a society girl experimenting with Communism.

McKenney, Ruth. Jake Home. Harcourt, 1943. Picture
of the proletarian struggle from 1912 to the early
1930's; organization of labor, Communist activity, and
the Sacco-Vanzetti trial.

McMillion, Bonner. The Lot of Her Neighbors. Lippincott,
1953. Pictures the spirit of a Texas town in the Twenties.

Marks, Percy. Plastic Age. Century, 1924. Detailed
picture of all sides of college life in the post-war
years.

Maxwell, William. The Folded Leaf. Harper, 1945. Picture of high school life in Chicago in the early Twenties.

Meacher, Joseph William. Tippy Locklin. Little, 1960.
A story of boyhood and of Catholic family life in Brooklyn in the 1920's.

Millar, Margaret. It's All in the Family. Random, 1948.
Story of family life during the year 1925.

Moll, Elick. Memoir of Spring. Putnam, 1961. Reminis-
cences of a Jewish boyhood in Brooklyn in the post
World War I era; picture of immigrant workers in the
ladies clothing industry.

Morley, Christopher. Kitty Foyle. Lippincott, 1939. Story
of a girl growing up struggling against tradition in an
industrial section of Philadelphia in the 1920's and
1930's.

--- Pandora Lifts the Lid. Doran, 1924. Adventurous
tale of a group of school girls who kidnap a financier
and a radical professor; a story of the flapper age.

Morris, Wright. The Huge Season. Viking, 1954. Pictures
the problems of the generation of the jazz age, told in
flashbacks from the viewpoint of the protagonists in
1952.

Nathan, Robert. One More Spring. Knopf, 1933. Effect of
the financial crash of 1929 on a diverse group who
spend the winter in a tool shed in Central Park.

Neff, Wanda Fraiden. Lone Voyagers. Houghton, 1929.
Story of economic hardships faced by the faculty of a
Midwestern university.

Nichols, Edward. Danger! Keep Out. Houghton, 1943.
Story of the gas and oil industry in Chicago in the
Twenties pictures the growth of the automobile industry and conflict between the workers and the industrial
plant.

Norris, Charles G. Pig Iron. Dutton, 1926. A criticism

of American society of the period following the first
world war; the theme is the effect of industralism on
human relations.

Pascal, Ernest. Cynthia Codentry. Brentano, 1926. Biographical novel of a young woman of the jazz age, set
in Long Island and Florida; a satire on the society of
the period.

Paterson, Isabel. Golden Vanity. Morrow, 1934. New
York City before and during the crash of 1929.

Perretta, Armando   Take a Number. Morrow, 1957.
Happy story of boyhood and family life in the Italian
section of Hartford, Connecticut.

Pratt, Theodore. The Barefoot Mailman. Duell, 1943.
Picture of the early Florida land booms and politics
in and around Palm Beach and Miami.

Prouty, Olive Higgins. Lisa Vale. Houghton, 1938. Boston in 1929 is the setting of a story about the social
and economic problems of a middle aged woman and
her four grown children.

Riesenberg, Felix. East Side, West Side. Harcourt, 1927.
Story of the rise of the main character from poverty
on the East Side to a position of wealth and power,
and the growth of New York City.

Rogers, Samuel. Dusk at the Grove. Little, 1934.
Scenes in the lives of three young people as they grow
up in the Twenties.

Rylee, Robert. St. George of Weldon. Farrar, 1937.
Thirty years in the life of a man who is drowned in
1929.

Sachs, Emanie N. Talk. Harper, 1924. Story of an in-
     secure marriage threatened by sudden wealth and a
     flapper dominated society.

Shenkin, Elizabeth. Midsummer's Nightmare. Rinehart,
     1960. Story of family life at a New York beach re-
     sort in 1923.

Siebel, Julia. For the Time Being. Harcourt, 1961. Fam-
     ily life in a small town in Kansas in the Post-World
     War I years.

Sinclair, Harold. Music Out of Dixie. Rinehart, 1952.
     Story of the growth of jazz music in the Twenties,
     from New Orleans' Storyville district to the success
     of Jelly Roll Morton in New York.

Sinclair, Upton. Another Pamela; or, Virtue Still Rewarded.
     Viking, 1950. Satire on the social history of the U. S.
     in the Twenties.

---  Between Two Worlds. Viking, 1941. Political and
     economic developments in post-war Europe and Amer-
     ica from 1919 to 1929; Treaty of Versailles, the rise
     of Mussolini in Italy, growing Nazi power in Germany,
     and the stock market crash in 1929. One of author's
     Lanny Budd series (see other categories.)

---  Boston. Boni, 1928. Story of the Sacco-Vanzetti
     trial; condemns the state of mind which permitted their
     conviction and execution.

---  Oil. Boni, 1927. Oil industry in Southern California,
     based on the Teapot Dome oil scandals during the
     Harding administration.

---  The Wet Parade. Farrar, 1931. Passionate defense

of prohibition showing the evil effects of alcohol, the
ineffective methods of prohibition agents, and the efforts
of the respectable rich to circumvent the law.

Smith, Betty.  Tomorrow Will Be Better.  Harper, 1948.
Typical family life in Brooklyn in the Twenties.

Soles, Gordon H.  Cornbread and Milk.  Doubleday, 1959.
Family and boy life on a Kansas farm during the
1920's.

Sorensen, Virginia.  On This Star.  Reynal, 1946. Story of
Mormon life in Utah in the Twenties.

Sprague, Jesse Rainsford.  The Middleman.  Morrow, 1929.
Story of the wholesale merchandising business and its
place in the economic system.

Sterrett, Frances Roberta.  The Golden Stream.  Penn,
1931.  Story of a wealthy family in conflict with a
son's wife until her common sense saves them in the
financial crash of 1929.

Stone, Alma.  The Harvard Tree.  Houghton, 1954. Story
of a happy family life and amiable race relations in a
small Texas town.

Stribling, T. S.  Backwater.  Doubleday, 1930. Social and
business life in an Arkansas rural community.

---   The Unfinished Cathedral.  Doubleday, 1934.  The real
estate boom, and a skyscraper cathedral project in a
North Alabama town.  Sequel to "The Store" (Nation
Grows Up).

Suckow, Ruth.  The Folks.  Farrar, 1934.  Family life in
a small Iowa town from World War I through the
Twenties.

Suhl, Yuri.  Cowboy on a Wooden Horse.  Macmillan, 1953.
     Continues the story of a Jewish boy and his problems,
     from courtship to labor unions.  Sequel to "One Foot
     in America."

---   One Foot in America.  Macmillan, 1950.  Humorous
     story of a Jewish boy and his father, immigrants from
     Poland; the son becoming Americanized, the father
     clinging to the old ways.

Tarkington, Booth.  Claire Ambler.  Doubleday, 1928.
     Social life and customs in the jazz age of the 1920's;
     picture of contemporary flapper society.

---   Mirthful Haven.  Doubleday, 1930.  Life in a small
     village in Maine as seen by the daughter of the local
     rum runner.

Thielen, Benedict.  The Lost Men.  Appleton, 1946. Story
     of World War I veterans given the job of building a
     road across the Florida Keys.

Train, Arthur Cheney.  The Needle's Eye.  Scribner, 1924.
     A story of labor union activity in the West Virginia
     coal fields.  Minor character is society girl with
     socialistic ideas.

---   Paper Profits.  Liveright, 1930.  Plea against stock
     market speculation.

Updegraff, Robert Rawls.  Captains in Conflict. Shaw, 1927.
     Story of the change in business methods from the turn
     of the century to the Twenties as two men compete
     for control of the company they founded together.

Walker, Charles Rumford.  Bread and Fire.  Houghton,
     1927.  A thesis novel dealing with the problems of la-

bor in the steel mill and the growth of the Socialist
movement.

Watts, Mary Stanbery.  The Fabric of the Loom.  Macmillan,
1924.  A story depicting the superficial aspects of
materialistic American society in contrast with European culture.

Webber, Gordon.  Years of Eden.  Little, 1951.  Story of
a boy growing up in Michigan in the Twenties.

Webster, Henry Kitchell.  An American Family.  Bobbs,
1923.  Story of contemporary family in Chicago in the
post-war years and the early Twenties.

Welty, Eudora.  Delta Wedding.  Harcourt, 1946.  Story of
the week before the wedding of one of the girls of a
Mississippi Delta family in 1923.

Wharton, Edith.  Twilight Sleep.  Appleton, 1927.  Novel
of social life in the upper levels of society; picture of
the optimism and self-indulgence of the jazz age.

Widdemer, Margaret.  Gallant Lady.  Harcourt, 1926.
Story of flippant irresponsibility among the young married set in the jazz age.

Wiley, John.  The Education of Peter.  Stokes, 1924. Story
of undergraduate life at Yale in the Twenties.

---   Queer Street.  Scribner, 1928.  Set in New York City,
the story of an old family house encroached on by
night clubs, speakeasies, and rooming houses.

Williamson, Thames Rose.  Hunky.  Coward, 1929. Slav
laborer in a big city, buffeted by a system he cannot
understand; social study of a workingman's life in the
Twenties.

Wilson, Mary B. Yesterday's Promise.  Penn, 1934. The
    effect of the 1929 market crash on the country club
    set.

Wilson, Mitchell.  My Brother, My Enemy.  Little, 1952.
    Story of early experiments with television.

Zugsmith, Leane.  Never Enough.  Liveright, 1932. Por-
    trays the extravagance, restlessness, and lack of pur-
    pose that characterized most of American life in the
    Twenties.

## The Nineteen-Thirties

Novels dealing with the decade of the nineteen-thirties in United States history cover a wide range of dissimilar themes: The Depression and New Deal relief measures; labor union activity; the rise of Nazism and fascism and the approach of war; and contemporary family life in which one of the larger issues of the period is used as a background. Another theme unique to this period and closely related to the rise of fascism in its social implications deals with local politics and demagogery, as exemplified, for example, by the rise to power of Huey Long in Louisiana.

Algren, Nelson. A Walk on the Wild Side. Farrar, 1956. Story of degenerate life in New Orleans during the Depression.

Atherton, Gertrude. House of Lee. Appleton, 1940. Effect of the Depression on the women of an upper class San Francisco family.

Bell, Thomas. All Brides are Beautiful. Little, 1936. Story of a young couple living in the Bronx during the Depression on $25 a week, who determine to be happy in their marriage, and succeed.

Blackwell, Louise. The Men Around Hurley. Vanguard, 1957. Story of life in a remote small town in Alabama from the time of the Depression, through the 1930's, to the outbreak of World War II.

Boyd, Thomas Alexander. In Time of Peace, Minton, 1935.

192

Story of a white-collar worker, embittered by the effects of the Depression, who turns to radicalism when
he is forced into the laboring class.

Breckenridge, Gerald. The Besieged. Doubleday, 1937.
Effect of the Depression on the character of the members of several different families.

Brody, Catherine. Nobody Starves. Longmans, 1932.
Story of the Depression among automobile factory
workers in and around Detroit.

Browne, Lewis. See What I Mean? Random, 1943. Rise
of a subversive movement in Southern California in
the late thirites; anti-Semitism used as a tool by Nazi
sympathizers.

Brush, Katharine. Don't Ever Leave Me. Farrar, 1935.
Picture of the hard-drinking, fast living country club
set with the fashions, catch-words, and songs of 1932.

Buckles, Eleanor. Valley of Power. Creative Age, 1945.
Story of TVA, its value and meaning, and the reaction
of the Tennessee mountain families who must be evicted to make way for it.

Burnett, William Riley. King Cole. Harper, 1936. Picture
of state politics, set around the last six days in a
gubernatorial campaign in which the honest governor
resorts to a planned riot to help him win re-election.

Caldwell, Janet Taylor. Eagles Gather. Scribner, 1940.
Brings the story of a Pennsylvania munitions family up
to 1938. Sequel to "Balance Wheel" (World War I).

Callaghan, Morley. They Shall Inherit the Earth. Random,
1935. Effects of the Depression on a group of people

in a moderate sized American city.

Carousso, Dorothee. Open Then the Door. Morrow, 1942.
Story of a happy marriage in spite of mothers-in-law
and the Depression.

Corey, Paul. Acres of Antaeus. Holt, 1946. The plight
of the farmers when foreclosures and eviction threat-
ened during the hard years of the 1930's.

Corrigan, Barbara. Voyage of Discovery. Scribner, 1945.
Sophisticated picture of college life in the 1930's.

Covert, Alice. The Months of Rain. Kinsey, 1941. Oklahoma farm family fights droughts, storms, and the
Depression.

--- Return to Dust. Kinsey, 1939. Dust bowl conditions
and the reaction to government relief in a small Oklahoma community.

Curran, Dale. Piano in the Band. Reynal, 1940. Story of
the feverish atmosphere of the world of jazz music in
1933.

Curry, Peggy. Oil Patch. McGraw, 1959. Story of life
in a Western oil town in the 1930's; wife rebels against
strict company rule.

Davis, Julia. The Sun Climbs Slow. Dutton, 1942. America at the time of the Spanish Civil War.

Davis, Kenneth. The Years of the Pilgrimage. Doubleday,
1948. Conflicting philosophies in a Kansas town in the
Thirties.

Deal, Bordon. Dunbar's Cove. Scribner, 1957. Study of
the social and economic life in the Tennessee River

valley in the Thirties; a family's fight with TVA over condemnation of their land for a dam.

Deasy, Mary. Devil's Bridge. Little, 1952. Politics in a Southern town; 1929-1933.

Dos Passos, John. Grand Design. Houghton, 1949. Story of New Deal politics in Washington.

--- Number One. Houghton, 1943. Politics and the gullibility of the masses in a story of a Southern demagogue; based on the career of Huey Long.

Ellison, Earl. The Dam. Random, 1941. Story of the construction of a W.P.A. dam near Chicago and its effect on the chief engineer.

Ellison, Ralph. Invisible Man. Random, 1952. Story of a Negro trying to find himself and of Negro-white relations during the Depression years. Set in a small Southern town and in New York's Harlem.

Ethridge, Willie Snow. Mingled Yarn. Macmillan, 1938. Story of a paternalistic Georgia mill owner; welfare plan and social clubs offered as compensation for starvation wages.

Faulkner, John. Men Working. Harcourt, 1941. Story of a shiftless family who leave tenant farming to go to work for the W.P.A.

Feibleman, Peter S. A Place Without Twilight. World, 1958. Negro life in New Orleans in the 1930's and 1940's.

Gallagher, Thomas. The Gathering Darkness. Bobbs, 1952. Follows the economic ups and downs of a middle class family in New York; 1929-1942.

Gilbreth, Frank B.  Loblolly.  Crowell, 1959.  Warm and
    funny story of an eccentric family in Charleston, South
    Carolina in 1935, bringing in the Depression and the
    New Deal as background.

Gold, Herbert.  Therefore Be Bold.  Dial, 1960.  Story of
    a Jewish boy growing up in a non-Jewish suburb of
    Cleveland, Ohio in the 1930's.

Granit, Arthur.  Time of the Peaches.  Abelard, 1959.
    Poetic story of Jewish life in the Brownsville section
    of Brooklyn in the 1930's.

Halper, Albert.  The Chute.  Viking, 1937.  Proletarian
    novel set in the order department of a Chicago mailing
    house; theme is the inhuman activity needed to keep
    the package chute fed.

---  Union Square.  Viking, 1933.  Story of a few days in
    the life of the radicals and the destitute in the tene-
    ments in the Union Square area of New York.

Hamilton, Harry.  River Song.  Bobbs, 1945.  Story of two
    Mississippi River bums after a radio scout discovers
    their musical talent.

Herbst, Josephine.  Rope of Gold.  Harcourt, 1939. Continues
    the story of a middle class American family through
    the Depression; 1933-1937.  Sequel to "The Execution-
    er Waits" (Twenties).

Heyward Du Bose.  Star Spangled Virgin.  Farrar, 1939.
    Story of the Virgin Islands; showing the disintegrating
    effect of New Deal relief measures on the natives.

Hicks, Granville.  Only One Storm.  Macmillan, 1942.
    World events from 1937 to 1939 as seen by a family

who retreated from the pressures of New York City
business life.

Hobart, Alice Tisdale. The Cup and the Sword. Bobbs,
1942. Story of the California grape and wine indus-
tries from the 1920's to the beginning of World War II.

Hubbell, Catherine. Frances. Norton, 1950. Picture of
life in New York City from the 1920's to the 40's.

Hueston, Ethel. A Roof Over Their Heads. Bobbs, 1937.
Picture of moral disintegration brought on by the Depression; theme is that unemployment forced families
together in overcrowded conditions and going on relief
was inevitable.

Hull, Morris. Cannery Anne. Houghton, 1936. Picture of
life among the migratory workers in a California cannery.

Idell, Albert. The Corner Store. Doubleday, 1953. Family
life in a run down section of Philadelphia during the
Depression.

Jackson, Margaret. Kindy's Crossing. Bobbs, 1934. Story
of the rise and fall of an American industrialist family
from wealth and power in the automobile industry to
the loss of everything during the Depression.

Jackson, Shirley. The Road Through the Wall. Farrar,
1948. Picture of American middle class family life
in a California town in 1936.

Janeway, Elizabeth. Leaving Home. Doubleday, 1953.
Story of the insecurity of three children growing up
in Brooklyn in the 1930's.

Johnson, Josephine. Jordanstown. Simon and Schuster,

1937. Story of the hopelessness of the poor in a small
town contrasted with the indifference of the financially
secure.

--- Now in November. Simon and Schuster, 1934. Story
of poor crops, labor troubles, drought, and debt on a
Midwestern farm in the years leading up to the Depression.

Jones, Nard. Still to the West. Dodd, 1946. Building of
the Grand Coulee Dam on the Columbia River.

Kanin, Garson. Blow Up A Storm. Random, 1959. Story
centers around the members, white and Negro, of a
small jazz combo in the day of jazz music in the early
Thirties.

Kaufman, Charles. Fiesta in Manhattan. Morrow, 1939.
Story of a Mexican couple lured to New York; stranded
by unemployment in the Depression they turn to the
marihuana racket.

Keyes, Frances Parkinson. All That Glitters. Messner,
1941. Picture of social changes in Washington during
the period from December 1927 to June 1940.

Kroll, Harry Harrison. The Usurper. Bobbs, 1941. Conflict between the growers and the sharecroppers of
the South through prosperity and the Depression.

Langley, Adria Locke. A Lion is in the Streets. Whittlesey,
1945. Rise and fall of a demagogue; based on the
career of Huey Long.

Lanham, Edwin. The Stricklands. Little, 1939. Story of
the conflict centering around organizing the tenant
farmers of Oklahoma into unions after the Depression

had changed the system of owner-operated farms.

--- Thunder in the Earth. Harcourt, 1941. Story of a
Texas oil town in the 1930's; emphasizes that rich
natural resources should not be exploited.

Lawrence, Josephine. But You Are Young. Little, 1940.
Economic struggles of a young girl forced to support
her family through the Depression years.

--- If I Have Four Apples. Stokes, 1935. Story of a
middle-class family trying to live beyond their income
in spite of the Depression and of the inevitable consequences of installment buying.

--- No Stone Unturned. Little, 1941. Picture of the moral and economic standing of an ordinary American
family during the Depression and the recovery.

--- Sound of Running Feet. Stokes, 1937. Effects of the
Depression on the staff of a real estate office; picture
of home and office life during the period.

Lee, Harper. To Kill a Mockingbird. Lippincott, 1960.
Two children growing up in Alabama in the Thirties
witness small town life and violence when their lawyer
father defends a falsely accused Negro.

Lewis, Janet. Against a Darkening Sky. Doubleday, 1943.
Family life in the Santa Clara valley near San Francisco during the Depression.

Lewis, Sinclair. Ann Vickers. Doubleday, 1933. Social
satire of a professional feminist, social worker, and
prison reformer.

Linn, James Weber. Winds Over the Campus. Bobbs,
1936. Picture of students and faculty life at the Uni-

versity of Chicago.

Longstreet, Stephen. Decade, 1929-1939. Random, 1940.
Story of the financial decline of a benevolent old cap-
italist, from the crash of 1929 to the years preceding
World War II.

McIntyre, John Thomas. Ferment. Farrar, 1937. Proletarian novel of strike-breaking and labor racketeer-
ing in Philadelphia; theme is the futility of the workingman's struggle against the evils of industralism
and fascism.

--- Steps Going Down. Farrar, 1936. Novel of under-
world life in an American city of the Thirties.

McKay, Allis. Goodbye, Summer. Macmillan, 1953. Teen-
ager grows from adolescence on an apple rance on the
Columbia River near Seattle to manhood working on
the Grand Coulee Dam.

MacLeish, Archibald. Cone of Silence. Houghton, 1944.
Story of the United States in the summer of 1933; the
growth of fascism in Europe and America.

Maltz, Albert. The Underground Stream. Little, 1940.
Industrial conflict between Communists and organized
labor on one hand and fascists on the other.

Martin, Peter. The Building. Little, 1960. Story of a
Russian Jewish family struggling through the Depression years.

Mayhall, Jane. Cousin to Human. Harcourt, 1960. Story
of the maturing of a 15 year old girl in a small town
in Kentucky in the mid-Thirites.

Merrick, Elliott. From This Hill Look Down. Stephen Daye,

1934. Sketches of life in Vermont during the Depression; drought, rain, sick neighbors, and a CWA job make up part of the story.

Moore, Ruth. Spoonhandle. Morrow, 1946. Maine coastal town in the middle Thirties.

Morris, Hilda. The Main Stream. Putnam, 1939. Contrasting picture of life on a farm in New York and life in a factory town.

Newhouse, Edward. You Can't Sleep Here. Furman, 1934. Story centering around the movement for unemployment insurance; a New York reporter joins a squatters' colony and becomes active in the movement after losing his job during the Depression.

Norris, Charles. Flint. Doubleday, 1944. Conflict between capital and labor in the shipbuilding industry in San Francisco in the mid-Thirties.

--- Hands, Farrar, 1935. Novel showing how the Depression forced many to go back to the pioneer ways of working with the hands.

North, Jessica Nelson. Arden Acres. Harcourt, 1935. Story of a family in a slum section of Chicago on relief during the Depression.

Paul, Elliot. The Stars and Stripes Forever. Random, 1939. Paternalistic owner opposes the organization of a labor union in his factory.

Pierce, Noel. The Second Mrs. Draper. McBride, 1937. Social life among the Long Island sophisticated country club set in the Thirties.

Raymond, Margaret Thomsen. Bend in the Road. Longmans,

1934. Story of a young girl who leaves home and gets a job in a factory.

--- Sylvia, Inc. Dodd, 1938. Story of a young girl called home from art school to help her father save his failing pottery business during the Depression.

Rice, Elmer. Imperial City. Appleton, 1937. Complex social and financial life of a wealthy family in New York City.

Ritner, Ann Katherine. Seize a Nettle. Lippincott, 1961. Story of a household of women and of their efforts to keep going during the Depression.

Roberts, Marta. Tumbleweeds. Putnam, 1940. Unemployment and gradual demoralization of a Mexican couple brought to California as railroad laborers; depicts the fear and dislike of relief agencies by those who need it most.

Robinson, Dorothy. The Diary of a Suburban Housewife. Morrow, 1936. Story of a Long Island housewife's courage and resourcefullness in meeting the Depression.

Roe, Wellington. The Tree Falls South. Putnam, 1937. Kansas farmers facing destitution from drought, dust, storms, and the Depression march on the county seat for government aid.

Rubin, Louis. The Golden Weather. Atheneum, 1961. Nostalgic view of a 13 year old boy's activities in Charleston, South Carolina before and during the 75th anniversary of the fall of Fort Sumter in 1936.

Sandoz, Mari. Capital City. Little, 1939. Picture of sordid political and social life in a Midwestern city;

story of conflict between capital and labor; the rise of
fascism, the tragedy of dispossessed farmers, unemployment, and graft and corruption in government.

Saxton, Alexander. The Great Midland. Appleton, 1948.
Economic class struggle and race relations in Chicago
in the Thirties; a story of labor unions, race riots,
and Communist activities.

Scott, Evelyn. Bread and a Sword. Scribner, 1937. Story
of a writer compromising his creative integrity to support his family during the Depression.

Scott, Virgil. The Hickory Stick. Swallow, 1948. Economic conditions of a young student and teacher in a
small Ohio town through the Depression years.

Scowcroft, Richard. First Family. Houghton, 1950. Life
in a prosperous middle-class family after the 1929
crash.

Simon, Charlie May. Share-Cropper. Dutton, 1937. Picture of the economic problems of an Arkansas cotton
farmer during the Depression; story of the tenant
farmers union.

Sims, Marian. The City on the Hill. Lippincott, 1940.
City solicitor of a small Southern city crusades
against slums, political graft, and unjust liquor regula-
tions.

Sinclair, Upton. Co-op. Farrar, 1936. Development of
the farmers' self-help co-operatives in California,
1932-1936.

---Dragon's Teeth. Viking, 1942. Period between 1929
and 1934; events in France and Germany during the

rise of Hitler, Goering, and Goebbels. Imprisonment
in Dachau prison; Lanny Budd series. Sequel to "Between Two Worlds" (1920's).

--- Presidential Agent. Viking, 1944. Lanny Budd becomes a secret agent of President Roosevelt reporting
on the political situation in Europe from 1937 to 1938
and the Munich Pact between Chamberlain and Hitler.
Sequel to "Wide Is the Gate" (below).

--- Wide Is the Gate. Viking, 1943. Lanny Budd furthers
his anti-Nazi activities while posing as a personal
friend of Hitler, Goering, and Hess, and witnesses
the beginning of the Spanish Civil War. Sequel to
"Dragon's Teeth" (above).

Skidmore, Hubert. The Hawk's Nest. Doubleday, 1941.
Senate investigation of the deaths of many workers
from silica dust on a West Virginia mountain tunnel
project in 1931.

Slade, Caroline. Job's House. Vanguard, 1941. Story of
unemployment and relief during Depression years.

--- The Triumph of Willie Pond. Vanguard, 1940. Ironic
story of a family on relief; thesis is that New Deal
relief measures treat symptoms rather than causes.

Smitter, Wessel. F.O.B. Detroit. Harper, 1938. Story
of the automobile industry showing the inhuman speed-
up in the factory and the workingman's helplessness
in the system.

Steinbeck, John. The Grapes of Wrath. Viking, 1939.
Story of Oklahoma farm families seeking relief from
the dust bowl by following the seasonal fruit picking

jobs in California.

--- In Dubious Battle. Viking, 1936. Story of a strike among the fruit pickers in the California fruit country during the Depression.

--- Of Mice and Men. Covici, 1937. Life of itinerant ranch workers in California.

Storm, Hans Otto. Count Ten. Longmans, 1940. Story of an American trying to find his place in life during the Depression.

Stribling, T. S. The Sound Wagon. Doubleday, 1935. Novel of politics; reform candidates opposed to the entrenched political machine and gangsters.

Taber, Gladys. A Star to Steer By. Macrae, 1938. Wisconsin mill town torn by a strike when a labor organizer incites the workers against the paternalistic mill owners.

Tarkington, Booth. The Heritage of Hatcher Ide. Doubleday, 1941. Pictures the changes in a respectable Middle West family as a result of the Depression.

Thomas, Dorothy. The Home Place. Knopf, 1936. Story of a family conflict and hope for better times when drought and the Depression force three brothers to return with their families to the old farm.

Trilling, Lionel. The Middle of the Journey. Viking, 1947. Life among the summer residents and natives in a farming area in Connecticut in the late 1930's; agitated by community feeling against a Communist in their midst.

Tunis, John. Son of the Valley. Morrow, 1949. Story of

TVA and the resentment of the people whose homes would be flooded by the project.

Turpin, Waters Edward. O Canaan! Doubleday, 1939. Follows the lives of the Negroes who migrated to Chicago in 1916 and after; through prosperity, the crash of 1929, and the Depression.

Villarreal, Jose Antonio. Pocho. Doubleday, 1959. Childhood of a Mexican migratory worker in the Santa Clara valley of California during the Depression years.

Vogel, Joseph. Man's Courage. Knopf, 1938. Technicalities and red tape of the New Deal relief system and the chaotic economic conditions faced by a Polish immigrant family in a small American city.

Wagner, Tobias. The Turbulent Pendrayles. Little, 1937. Family and social life of a Philadelphia locomotive manufacturer after the 1929 crash.

Walker, Mildred. Fireweed. Harcourt, 1934. Story of life in a lumber mill town in upper Michigan after the Depression closes the mill.

Warren, Robert Penn. All the King's Men. Harcourt, 1946. Story of a demagogue based on the life and death of Huey Long.

Weaver, John. Another Such Victory. Viking, 1948. Presents both sides of the veterans' Bonus March against Washington in 1932. MacArthur and Patton appear.

Webber, Gordon. What End But Love. Little, 1959. Memories of farm life and industrial growth set in the framework of a family reunion on a Michigan farm near the automobile factories in 1934.

Weller, George Anthony. Not to Eat, Not for Love. Smith
    and Haas, 1933. Picture of undergraduate life at Har-
    vard University in 1933.

Wickenden, Dan. The Red Carpet. Morrow, 1952. New
    York in 1936 as a young Illinois college graduate
    found it.

--- Tobias Brandywine. Morrow, 1948. A story of fam-
    ily life during nine years of the Depression and New
    Deal relief measures

Williams, Ben Ames. Time of Peace. Houghton, 1942.
    Novel of American life and political thought from
    1930 to Pearl Harbor; theme is the changing reaction
    to the threat of war and the gradual acceptance of
    Roosevelt's foreign policy.

Wolfe, Thomas. You Can't Go Home Again. Harper, 1940.
    Observations on events in the 1930's in New York,
    Brooklyn, England and Germany.

Wright, Richard. Native Son. Harper, 1940. Story of the
    frustrations and resentment in the life of a young
    Negro in Chicago in the 1930's.

Zara, Louis. Some for the Glory. Bobbs, 1937. Rise of
    orphan boy to presidential candidacy; details of ward,
    state, and national politics.

Zugsmith, Leane. Time To Remember. Random, 1936.
    Story of the conflicts involved in a department store
    strike, from the standpoint of the striking clerks.

# World War II

United States participation in World War II has been covered in almost all its phases by the fiction dealing with that period of our history. In addition to novels concerned with specific battles and with naval warfare in both theaters of operation - Europe and the Pacific - there are novels depicting various phases of the war on the home front and the plight of returning veterans. Among the themes developed in these novels are: American indifference to the war in Europe and the sharp reaction to the attack on Pearl Harbor; the treatment of Japanese-Americans in California internment camps; life in training camps and prisoner-of-war camps; the role of women in the war effort; the effect of the war on civilian life - the fear of invasion, civil defense measures, rationing and price controls; and the efforts of returning veterans to find their place in life under changed conditions and attitudes.

Adams, Frank Ramsay. When I Come Back. McBride, 1944. Story of a typical small town mother trying to keep her 17 year old son out of the army in 1942.

Allbrand, Martha. Without Orders. Little, 1943. Story of an American soldier in undercover work for the American army and the Italian underground.

Appel, Benjamin. Fortress in the Rice. Bobbs, 1951. Guerrilla warfare in the Philippines after Pearl Harbor.

Arnold, Elliott. The Commandos. Duell, 1942. Story of
the purpose, training, and action of the commando
guerrilla units culminating in a raid in Nazi-occupied
Norway.

--- Tomorrow Will Sing. Duell, 1945. Story of Italian-
American relations at a U. S. bomber base in Southern Italy.

--- Walk With the Devil. Knopf, 1950. Advance of the
American army in Italy.

Arnow, Harriette. The Dollmaker. Macmillan, 1954.
Story of a Kentucky family in wartime Detroit.

Arthur, Phyllis. Paying Guest. Samuel Curl, 1945. Conflicts among an unhappy family are straightened out by
their roomer, an engineer at the local war plant.

Ashmead, John. The Mountain and the Feather. Houghton,
1961. Story of wartime Hawaii and combat in the
South Pacific from 1943 to the Battle of Leyte Gulf.

Atwell, Lester. Private. Simon and Schuster, 1958.
Story of a middle-aged soldier in the Battle of the
Bulge and in the invasion of Germany.

August, John. Advance Agent. Little, 1942. A newspaperman and a soldier expose a secret Nazi organization.

Barr, George. Epitaph For an Enemy. Harper, 1958. An
American sergeant, leading a group of French vil-
lagers to the beach for evacuation, gains new understanding of the enemy as he sees the influence which
a humane German commander had on the group.

Beach, Edward. Run Silent, Run Deep. Holt, 1955. Realistic novel of submarine warfare in the Pacific.

Bergamini, David. The Fleet in the Window. Simon and
Schuster, 1960. Story of the guerrilla fighting in the
Philippines and life in a Japanese internment camp as
experienced by the young son of an American missionary doctor.

Beverley-Giddings, Arthur Raymond. Broad Margin. Morrow,
1945. An American flier, wounded with the RAF, re-
cuperates in Tidewater Virginia.

Bonner, Paul Hyde. Excelsior! Scribner, 1955. Scion of
a Swiss banking family faces conflicting loyalties in
America at the outbreak of the war.

Bowman, Peter. Beach Red. Random, 1945. Picture of
a landing assault on a Pacific island through the
thoughts and feelings of a soldier in the hour before
his death.

Boyle, Kay. His Human Majesty. Whittlesey, 1949. Ski
troopers training in Colorado in 1944.

Brelis, Dean. The Mission. Random, 1958. Story of an
OSS agent operating behind the Japanese lines in
Burma in 1943.

Bridge, Ann. A Place to Stand. Macmillan, 1953. Daughter of an American businessman becomes involved with
a family of Polish refugees and witnesses the brutality
of the Nazis when they march into Budapest in 1941.

Bright, Robert. The Life and Death of Little Jo. Doubleday, 1944. Story of the effect of the war on a young
Spanish-American from a village in New Mexico.

Brinkley, William. Don't Go Near the Water. Random,
1956. Comedy of a U. S. Navy public relations unit

on a Pacific island during the war.

Bromfield, Louis. Mr. Smith. Harper, 1951. An American major on a Pacific island reviews his fruitless life.

Brown, Eugene. The Locust Fire. Doubleday, 1957. Fast paced action story of an Air Transport Command pilot in China during World War II.

Brown, Harry. A Walk in the Sun. Knopf, 1944. Story of a squad of American soldiers on a beachhead in Italy.

Brown, Joe David. Kings Go Forth. Morrow, 1956. Story of two American artillery observers in action against the Germans in Italy and Southern France.

Buck, Pearl. Command the Morning. Day, 1959. Story of the scientists who developed the first atomic chain reaction at the University of Chicago, December 2, 1942; set in Chicago, Oak Ridge, Washington, and Los Alamos.

Burnett, William Riley. Tomorrow's Another Day. Knopf, 1945. A gay young gambler returns from the war and settles down in the restaurant business.

Busch, Niven. They Dream of Home. Bobbs, 1944. Story of five U. S. Marines who face the problems of adjusting to civilian life in Los Angeles after action in the Pacific.

Caldwell, Janet Taylor. The Final Hour. Scribner, 1944. Conflict in the Pennsylvania munitions dynasty from 1939 to 1942; some want to do business with Hitler. Sequel to "Eagles Gather" (Thirties).

Calmer, Ned. The Strange Land. Scribner, 1950. Story of an unsuccessful Allied offensive in Europe in 1944.

Camerer, David. The Damned Wear Wings. Doubleday,
    1958. Personality conflicts among a group of U. S.
    pilots on an air base in Italy; bombing missions over
    the Ploesti oil fields.

Camp, William Martin. Retreat, Hell! Appleton, 1943.
    Story of the U. S. Marines fighting in Shanghai and at
    Cavite, Bataan, and Corregidor in the Philippines on
    December 6, 1941.

Camp, William Henry. Skip To My Lou. Doubleday, 1945.
    Story of an itinerant Arkansas Ozark hill family who
    migrate to the California ship yards during the war.

Carleton, Marjorie. The Swan Sang Once. Morrow, 1947.
    A soldier, released from Japanese prison camp, seeks
    proof that his wife was a traitor during the war.

Carse, Robert. From the Sea and the Jungle. Scribner,
    1951. Episode on an island in the West Indies in-
    volving an ex-gangster, German submarines and the
    sinking of American ships.

Chamales, Tom. Never So Few. Scribner, 1957. Guerrilla
    activity in Burma in World War II.

Chambliss, William C. Boomerang. Harcourt, 1944. Story
    of a new U. S. Navy ship in the South Pacific.

Chidester, Ann. No Longer Fugitive. Scribner, 1943.
    Story of a draft dodger whose experiences give him the
    conviction he needs to take his part in the war effort.

Clagett, John. The Slot. Crown, 1958. Story of a PT
    boat and its crew assigned to guard the busy channel
    between Guadalcanal and the Solomon Islands in World
    War II.

Cochrell, Boyd. The Barren Beaches of Hell. Holt, 1959.
   Story of a young Marine private through the invasions
   of Tarawa, Saipan, and Tinian and occupation duty at
   Nagasaki, Japan.

Connell, Evan S. The Patriot. Viking, 1960. Story of the
   training of a naval air cadet, of his life as a seaman,
   and of his post war art studies at the University of
   Kansas.

Cook, Fannie. Mrs. Palmer's Honey. Doubleday, 1946.
   Story of the war work and labor union activity of a
   lovable Negro girl in St. Louis.

Cotler, Gordon. Bottletop Affair. Simon and Schuster,
   1959. A humorous story of the search for a lone
   Japanese holdout on a small Pacific island during the
   war.

Covert, Alice. The Eternal Mountain. Doubleday, 1944.
   Romance in which a young man takes a job in a war
   plant and gets in shape for the army.

Cozzens, James. Guard of Honor. Harcourt, 1948. Tri-
   bulations of the commanding officer of an air base in
   Florida.

Davis, Clyde Brion. Playtime Is Over. Lippincott, 1949.
   Day-to-day life on a small Arkansas farm during the
   war.

--- The Stars Incline. Farrar, 1946. Career of a Denver newspaper man from the Spanish Civil War to the
   campaigns in Africa and Europe in World War II.

Davis, Paxton. Two Soldiers. Simon and Schuster, 1956.
   Two novelettes showing the war in the China-Burma-

India theater.

De Pereda, Prudencio. Windmills in Brooklyn. Atheneum,
1960. Story of a young boy growing up in the Spanish
colony of Brooklyn during the World War II years.

Dibner, Martin. The Deep Six. Doubleday, 1953. Life a-
board a Navy cruiser during the war.

Dixon, Clarice M. The Devil and the Deep. Scribner,
1944. Stories of life in the U. S. Merchant Marine
in 1941-1942.

Dodson, Kenneth. Away All Boats. Little, 1954. Amphi-
bious warfare in the Pacific from the campaigns in the
Gilbert Islands to Okinawa.

--- Stranger to the Shore. Little, 1956. Adventurous
story centered around a U. S. Merchant Marine sailor
and a German raider in the waters off Chile in 1942.

Dunlap, Katharine. Once There Was a Village. Morrow,
1941. Story of Americans involved in war mobilization
in a French village at the beginning of the war.

Edmiston, James. Home Again. Doubleday, 1955. Story of
Japanese-Americans in California and their life in re-
location camps during the war.

Ellison, James Whitfield. The Freest Man on Earth. Doubleday, 1958. Story of what happens when a conscientious
objector refuses to answer a call by the draft board.

Eyster, Warren. Far From the Customary Skies. Random,
1953. Life cycle of an American destroyer from training cruise through action at Guadalcanal and New
Guinea to its sinking in a battle.

Falstein, Louis. Face of a Hero. Harcourt, 1950. Story of

hate, fear, and boredom among the men who flew A-
merican bombers based in Italy.

Fast, Howard. The Winston Affair. Crown, 1959. Story
of the trial of an American soldier for the killing of a
British soldier in the Far East.

Fleming, Berry. Colonel Effingham's Raid. Duell, 1943.
Story of a retired army man and a young newspaper
man fighting local corrupt politics in a Georgia town
until the reporter joins the National Guard on the way
to war.

--- The Lightwood Tree. Lippincott, 1947. A Georgia
teacher, exempt from the draft, works to defend liberty
at home when local politicians use undemocratic action
in arresting a student.

Forester, C. S. The Good Shepherd. Little, 1955. Tale
of four U. S. Navy ships escorting a merchant marine
convoy from America to England in the face of repeated German submarine attacks.

Fosburgh, Hugh. View From the Air. Scribner, 1953.
Story of the crew of a bomber on forty missions over
Truk in the South Pacific.

Frizell, Bernard. Ten Days in August. Simon and Schuster,
1956. A romance set against the German occupation of
Paris, as the underground Resistance movement pre-
pares for the advancing Allies.

Frye, Pearl. The Narrow Bridge. Little, 1947. Story of
the tension and antagonism in Honolulu after the attack
on Pearl Harbor.

Gabriel, Gilbert Wolf. I Got a Country. Doubleday, 1944.

Story of three U. S. Army soldiers stationed in Alaska.

Gallico, Paul. The Lonely. Knopf, 1949. A young U. S. flyer must decide between an English girl and his girl back home.

Garth, David. Bermuda Calling. Putnam, 1944. Spy story of World War II.

--- Watch on the Bridge. Putnam, 1959. The capture of the Remagen Bridge over the Rhine in March, 1945, is the central element in a love story of an American soldier and a German girl.

Gilpatric, Guy. Action in the North Atlantic. Dutton, 1943. Action with the U. S. Merchant Marine on the run to Murmansk.

Gionannitti, Len. The Prisoners of Combine D. Holt, 1957. Story of six American airmen in a German prison camp in 1944-45.

Glaspell, Susan. Judd Rankin's Daughter. Lippincott, 1945. Story of wartime family life; a war-shocked son; isolationist editor in Iowa.

Goertz, Arthemise. Dream of Juji. McGraw, 1958. Story of a group of Americans interned in Japan at the outbreak of the war.

Goethals, Thomas. Chains of Command. Random, 1955. Strategists at the rear headquarters of a U. S. army unit ignore warnings of a German offensive shortly before the Battle of the Bulge.

Gwaltney, Francis Irby. The Day the Century Ended. Rinehart, 1955. Story of the brutality of the war in the Philippines which ended on the day the atom bomb was dropped at Hiroshima.

Haines, William Wister. Command Decision. Little, 1947.
The air war over Europe as seen by the commanding
officer of a bomber division based in England.

Hall, James Norman. Lost Island. Little, 1944. Pictures
the destriction of the natives' way of life when an army
of American experts prepare to build an airbase on a
small Pacific island.

Hawkins, John and Ward Hawkins. The Pilebuck. Dutton,
1943. Indictment of labor union racketeers and slack-
ers in a wartime shipyard in the Northwest where an
FBI spy is sent to investigate sabotage.

Haydn, Hiram. Manhattan Furlough. Bobbs, 1945. Story
of a young soldier, depressed over the death of a
friend in training camp, on leave in New York City.

Hayes, Alfred. Girl on the Via Flaminia. Harper, 1949.
The last year of the war in Italy; love affair between
an American G.I. and an Italian girl.

Heggen, Thomas. Mister Roberts. Houghton, 1946. Story
of life on a cargo ship in the Pacific and the reaction
of the crew to the dullness of their duty.

Hemingway, Leicester. The Sound of the Trumpet. Holt,
1953. Two American cameramen record the invasion
on the Normandy beaches on D-Day.

Herber, William. Tomorrow to Live. Coward, 1958. Set
in Hawaii and Saipan in 1944; story of the U. S. Marines engaged in island fighting.

Hersey, John. The War Lover. Knopf, 1959. Life of an

American Flying Fortress crew on missions and on a
bomber base in England.

Heyliger, William. Home is a One-Way Street. Westminster,
1945. Story of a wounded soldier and his problems in
readjusting to his wife, job, and family.

Heym, Stefan. The Crusaders. Little, 1948. Follows an
American division from the Normandy invasion through
France, Germany, the liberation of Paris, the Battle
of the Bulge, and the occupation of the Ruhr.

Hicks, Granville. Behold Trouble. Macmillan, 1944. Story
of a conscientious objector and the consequences of
his stand against the draft board.

Higginbotham, Robert E. Wine for my Brothers. Rinehart, 1946. Story of the trip of an oil tanker from
Texas to New York in January, 1942.

Hillyer, Laurie. Time Remembered. Macmillan, 1945.
Story of normal family life disrupted by the war when
a son is caught in the attack on Pearl Harbor; the
mother represents pacifist sentiment.

Hilton, James. Nothing So Strange. Little, 1947. Story of
a young American scientist viewing the war in Europe
and England.

---  The Story of Dr. Wassell. Little, 1943. Fictionized
account of the heroic efforts of Dr. Corydon Wassell
to rescue the wounded men from the H.M.S. Marblehead and lead them from Java to Australia in 1942.

Hoffman, William. The Trumpet Unblown. Doubleday,
1955. Experiences of an American soldier in a field
hospital during the Battle of the Bulge.

Hough, Henry Beetle. Rooster Crow in Town. Appleton,
    1945. A Maine coastal town during 1942-43 and the
    effect on the lives of the people of the fear of in-
    vasion, civil defense dimouts, a group of Amphibians
    practicing in the neighborhood, price control, ration-
    ing, and general war fever.

Howe, George. Call it Treason. Viking, 1949. Story of
    the training and action of three German prisoners
    dropped behind German lines as a U. S. Army intel-
    ligence team.

Hueston, Ethel. Mother Went Mad on Monday. Bobbs,
    1944. Family and home life in a small town in New
    York during the war; son reported missing, teen-age
    daughter has romance with an army flier.

Hunt, Howard. East of Farewell. Knopf, 1942. Story of
    a destroyer on convoy duty in the Atlantic.

--- Limit of Darkness. Random, 1944. Story of 24 hours
    in the lives of a group of American fliers based on
    Guadalcanal.

Jessey, Cornelia. Teach the Angry Spirit. Crown, 1949.
    Life in the Mexican quarter of Los Angeles during the
    war.

Jonas, Carl. Beachhead on the Wind. Little, 1945. Pic-
    ture of cleanup operations after a landing on a beach-
    head in the Aleutian Islands.

Jones, James. From Here to Eternity. Scribner, 1951.
    Pre-Pearl Harbor army life in Hawaii, ending with
    Japanese attack.

--- The Pistol. Scribner, 1958. Follows the actions of a

soldier who finds a pistol during the attack on Pearl
Harbor through the plots to take it from him.

Jones, Nard. The Island. Sloane, 1948. Pictures the
conditions and problems typical of American communities during the war in the story of three men in
Seattle.

Kadish, M. R. Point of Honor. Random, 1951. Story of
an American artillery battalion in the Italian campaign.

Kantor, MacKinlay. Glory for Me. Coward, 1945. Story
in verse form of three veterans with bitter war memories who find themselves misfits in their home town.

--- Happy Land. Coward, 1943. A father saddened by
news of his son's death reviews the boy's life.

Kehoe, Karon. City in the Sun. Dodd, 1946. Story of a
Japanese-American family in California and in a re-
location camp during the war.

Kendrick, Baynard H. Lights Out. Morrow, 1945. Reaction of a blinded soldier to his rehabilitation to
daily routine living, and to his discovery that two of
his new friends are a Negro and a Jew.

Keyes, Frances Parkinson. Also the Hills. Messner,
1943. Story of the war effort in a New Hampshire
village.

Klaas, Joe. Maybe I'm Dead. Macmillan, 1955. Story of
the forced march of 10,000 prisoners-of-war from a
German prison camp just before the liberation in 1945.

Knowles, John. A Seperate Peace. Macmillan, 1959. Story
of life at a New Hampshire boarding school in 1942,

showing the restlessness caused by the war.

Kolb, Avery. Jigger Witchet's War. Simon and Schuster, 1959. Humorous story of a Negro soldier in England and behind the German lines in France in World War II.

Kubeck, James. The Calendar Epic. Putnam, 1956. Life aboard a U. S. Merchant Marine ship in World War II; emphasis on amorous adventures during shore leave.

Lamott, Kenneth. The Stockade. Little, 1952. Pictures the inhuman treatment of 5,000 Okinawans and Koreans in an American prison camp on a Pacific island near the end of the war.

Landon, Joseph. Angle of Attack. Doubleday, 1952. Story of air warfare and the effects of an unethical act on the crew of a bomber based in Italy.

Lasswell, Mary. High Time. Houghton, 1944. Three beer drinking warmhearted old ladies contribute to the war effort.

Lawrence, Josephine. There Is Today. Little, 1942. A story of the wartime home front representing typical types: the young couple who marry in spite of the draft, the glory-seeking volunteer worker, and the middleaged patriotic veteran.

--- A Tower of Steel. Little, 1943. Story of women in wartime, represented by four young women who work in a law office.

Lay, Beirne and Sy Bartlett. Twelve O'clock High. Harper, 1948. Story of a demoralized bomber group based in England in 1942; pictures the strain and tension of the war in the air.

Leeming, John. It Always Rains in Rome. Farrar, 1961.
A lighthearted tale revolving around the question of
whether or not to destroy an ancient bridge in Italy.

Leonard, George. Shoulder the Sky. McDowell, 1959.
Story of two young flight instructors assigned to a
Georgia base instead of being sent into combat duty
in 1944; picture of the training of bomber pilots.

Lewisohn, Ludwig. Breathe Upon These. Bobbs, 1944.
Story of a typical American family shocked into a-
wareness of the world by the experiences of a German
refugee scientist.

Long, Margaret. Louisville Saturday. Random, 1950. Story
of eleven girls and the crises they meet one Saturday
night in Louisville, Kentucky in 1942.

Loomis, Edward. End of a War. Ballantine, 1957. Follows an infantryman from training in France, through
the Belgian offensive in the winter of 1944, and the
occupation of Germany.

MacCuish, David. Do Not Go Gentle. Doubleday, 1960.
Story of a young man who grows up in a Montana mining town; joins the Marine Corps, and after boot camp
survives the heavy fighting on Guadalcanal.

Mackay, Margaret. For All Men Born. John Day, 1943.
Story of life at Pearl Harbor on the day of the Japanese attack.

McLaughlin, Robert. The Side of the Angels. Knopf, 1947.
The reactions of two brothers to their army experiences in the Mediteranean area.

McLeish, Archibald and Robert De San Marzano. Infernal
      Machine. Houghton, 1947. Satire of official Washing-
      ton during the war.

Mailer, Norman. The Naked and the Dead. Rinehart, 1948.
      Picture of amphibious assault and jungle fighting in the
      capture of a Japanese-held island in the Pacific.

Marmur, Jacland. Andromeda. Holt, 1947. An American
      freighter, one of the last to leave Singapore before the
      Japanese arrive, carries a young romantic girl and
      an American who turns out to be a Japanese agent.

Marquand, J. P. Repent in Haste. Little, 1945. Story of
      the marital problems of a flier in the Pacific.

---   So Little Time. Little, 1943. Satire of the contem-
      porary scene of theatrical and literary life centering
      around a World War I veteran whose son is nearing
      draft age.

Master, Dexter. The Accident. Knopf, 1955. Novel about
      the making and using of the atomic bomb told during
      the eight days it takes a young atomic scientist to die
      from exposure to radiation; setting is Los Alamos in
      1946.

Matheson, Richard. The Beardless Warriors. Little, 1960
      Story of the battle experiences of a squad of U. S.
      riflemen made up chiefly of 18 year old replacements;
      set in Germany in December, 1944.

Mattiessen, Peter. Raditzer. Viking, 1961. Character
      study of two non-combatant sailors, set in Honolulu
      during World War II.

Mayo, Eleanor R. Turn Home. Morrow, 1945. Story of a

veteran trying to find a place in his home town.

Merrick, Gordon. The Strumpet Wind. Morrow, 1947.
Story of an American intelligence officer working with
the French underground.

Miller, Merle. Island 49. Crowell, 1945. Picture of the
home background and the action of a group of men
attacking a coral atoll in the Pacific.

Moon, Bucklin. The Darker Brother. Doubleday, 1943.
Story of a Southern Negro facing northern intolerance;
Pearl Harbor makes him aware of his country and he
goes willingly to fight for it.

Morris, Terry. No Hiding Place. Knopf, 1945. Story of
the problems faced by wives who follow their husbands
in the army.

Mydans, Shelley. The Open City. Doubleday, 1945. Picture of life in Santo Tomas prison camp at Manila
after the Japanese invaded the Philippines.

Myrer, Anton. The Big War. Appleton, 1957. Story of
the U. S. Marines in action in the Pacific, and in love
on the home front.

Nordhoff, Charles and Norman Hall. The High Barbaree.
Little, 1945. Iowa farm-boy pilot shot down in the
Pacific finds his dream island, but it is only in death
he has found his dream.

Ogilvie, Elisabeth. Ebbing Tide. Crowell, 1947. Bennett's
Island off the coast of Maine during the war. Sequel
to "Storm Tide" (below).

--- Storm Tide. Crowell, 1945. Life of lobster fisher-

men on an island off the Maine coast; the coming of
war brings the submarine menace. Sequel to "High
Tide at Noon."

O'Rourke, Frank. 'E' Company. Simon and Schuster, 1945.
Formation, training, and action of an infantry company
from December 17, 1941 to first action in Africa a
year later.

Paul, Louis. This Is My Brother. Crown, 1943. Story of
five U. S. soldiers, their thoughts and feelings, as
they await death as spies after capture by the Japanese.

Plagemann, Bentz. The Steel Cocoon. Viking, 1958. Story
of a ship and its crew at war in the Pacific.

Popkin, Zelda. The Journey Home. Lippincott, 1945. A
train wreck forces a combat veteran to reconsider his
ideas about the civilians with whom he had been traveling.

Powell, Richard. The Soldier. Scribner, 1960. Story of
the heroic evacuation of U. S. forces from a small
unstrategic island in the Pacific.

Pratt, Rex. You Tell My Son. Random, 1958. Story of
the annihilation of a Regular Army platoon during a
patrol action in the South Pacific and of the survivors'
efforts to whip the inexperienced Guard unit to which
they were assigned into shape for the coming battle.

Pratt, Theodore. Mr. Winkle Goes to War. Duell, 1943.
Humorous story of a hen-pecked husband who is drafted
and returns home a hero.

Ripperger, Henrietta. 112 Elm Street. Putnam, 1943.

Story of family life on the home front; father works in
a war plant, one son is in the army, and the family
is keeping a young English boy for the duration.

Rosenhaupt, Hans. The True Deceivers. Dodd, 1954.
Story of a German-born intelligence officer in the A-
merican army assigned the job of interrogating German prisoners of war.

Routsong, Alma. A Gradual Joy. Houghton, 1953. Story
of a World War II veteran and his ex-Wave wife, and
of their life in a trailer camp while attending Michigan
State College.

Rubinstein, S. Leonard. The Battle Done. Morrow, 1954.
Prisoners, guards, and camp personnel in a prisoner-
of-war-camp in South Carolina shortly after the war.

Rylee, Robert. The Ring and the Cross. Knopf, 1947.
Racial philosophies of democracy and fascism in a
Texas town during World War II.

Sapieha, Virgilia Peterson. Beyond This Shore. Lippincott,
1942. Story of an American girl married to a Polish
count who finds Americans indifferent to the Nazi
threat after fleeing the Germans in Austria and Poland.

Saroyan, William. The Human Comedy. Harcourt, 1943.
Story of family life in wartime; one son away in the
army and the young ones working at odd jobs.

Saxton, Alexander. Bright Web in the Darkness. St. Martins, 1958. Story of the San Francisco shipyards centering around the labor issues involving Negroes in
war work.

Shapiro, Lionel. Sixth of June. Doubleday, 1955. An Amer-

ican paratrooper and an English commander take part
in the D-Day invasion of Normandy.

Shaw, Charles. Heaven Knows, Mr. Allison. Crown, 1952.
After the fall of Bataan a nun and a marine are
marooned on an island behind Japanese lines.

Shaw, Irwin. The Young Lions. Random, 1948. Two A-
mericans and a German seen in their pre-war life and
in episodes of army training and on war duty.

Sheean, Vincent. A Certain Rich Man. Random, 1947.
Story of the wartime experiences, as a bomber pilot,
of a rich man and of its effect on his home life and
social responsibility after the war.

Sinclair. Upton. Dragon Harvest. Viking, 1945. Lanny
Budd in Europe as the secret agent of President
Roosevelt, meets Hitler and Chamberlain, and takes
part in the evacuation of Dunkirk. Sequel to "Presidential Agent" (The Thirties).

--- O Shepherd, Speak! Viking, 1949. Lanny Budd takes
part in the Nuremburg war trials in 1946, acts as
President Truman's representative in Moscow, and
uses his trust fund to promote world peace. Sequel
to "One Clear Call."

--- One Clear Call. Viking, 1948. Lanny Budd, as
Roosevelt's secret agent, operates in Italy, France,
Spain, and Germany from the invasion of Sicily to the
invasion of France; story ends with Roosevelt's re-
election in 1944. Sequel to "Presidential Mission."

--- Presidential Mission. Viking, 1947. Lanny Budd acts
as Roosevelt's secret agent in Africa before the A-

merican invasion, and later, in Germany. Sequel to
"A World To Win."

--- A World To Win. Viking, 1946. As agent of President Roosevelt, Lanny Budd reports on German plans
to attack Russia; is tutored by Einstein for a mission
to learn about German atomic energy research, and
lands in Hong Kong at the outbreak of the war with
Japan; 1940-1942. Sequel to "Dragon's Harvest"
(above).

Sire, Glen. The Deathmakers. Simon and Schuster, 1960.
Story of war and death during General Patton's ar-
mored battalion push into Bavaria in the last days of
the war.

Skidmore, Hobert Douglas. Valley of the Sky. Houghton,
1944. Story of the experiences of a youthful bomber
crew in the South Pacific.

Slaughter, Frank. A Touch of Glory. Army medical officer returns home to find an industrial boom town;
forms group medicine plan in opposition to a compensation racket.

Sparks, Dorothy Elizabeth. Nothing As Before. Harper,
1944. Isolationist sympathies in a small Illinois town
shattered by the attack on Pearl Harbor.

Statham, Leon. Welcome, Darkness. Crowell, 1950.
Guerrilla warfare in the Philippines.

Stein, Gertrude. Brewsie and Willie. Random, 1946. Post-
war responsibilities of young Americans brought out in
the form of bull sessions among a group of soldiers in
France after the armistice.

Stong, Philip. One Destiny. Reynal, 1942. Story of a rural I-
owa community awakening to world events; farmer's
son gives up his medical education to become a pilot.

Syers, William Edward. The Seven. Duell, 1960. Story of
the action of a U. S. Navy submarine chaser off the
coast of Central America and in the Pacific.

Taylor, Ward. Roll Back the Sky. Holt, 1956. Story of a
member of a B-29 bombing crew based on Saipan.
Tense picture of low level bombing missions over
Japan.

Thatcher, Russell. The Captain. Macmillan, 1951. Pressures and frustrations of the commander of a landing
craft in the Pacific.

Tillett, Dorothy. Angry Dust. Doubleday, 1946. Story of
conflict between management and labor in a metal
working plant in New York where the C.I.O. is trying
to strengthen its position.

Tregaskis, Richard. Stronger Than Fear. Random, 1945.
Picture of street fighting tactics in the story of an
army patrol clearing out Nazi snipers.

Uris, Leon. Battle Cry. Putnam, 1953. Life among the
Marines at Guadalcanal, Tarawa, and Saipan.

Van de Water, Frederic. The Sooner To Sleep. Duell,
1946. Story of women without men in a Vermont town
during the war.

Van Praag, Van. Day Without End. Sloane, 1949. Story
of an exhausted platoon in the hedgerows of Normandy.

Wallace, Francis. Explosion. Morrow, 1943. Story of
the heroism of men trapped in a mine explosion and

of retribution when the Nazi agent responsible for the
explosion is identified.

Warrick, LaMar. Yesterday's Children. Crowell, 1943.
Story of a family with a draft-age son in college as
the war approaches; set in a suburb of Chicago.

Wendt, Lloyd. A Bright Tomorrow. Bobbs, 1945. Pacifist sentiment in rural South Dakota in 1940-1941.

Wernick, Robert. The Freebooters. Scribner, 1949. Adventures of three soldiers in an American unit in North
Africa and Italy.

White, Theodore. The Mountain Road. Sloane, 1958. Story
of an American demolition squad assigned to delay a
Japanese advance in China in 1944.

Wilder, Margaret. Since You Went Away. Whittlesey,
1943. Letters from a wife to her soldier husband
telling of life on the home front.

Wilhelm, Gale. The Time Between. Morrow, 1942. Story
of the ten days leave of an heroic American flyer
after hospitalization before he returns to the war.

Williams, George. The Blind Bull. Abelard, 1952. An A-
merican major in a Saipan hospital reviews his past
life and his battle experiences.

Williams, Wirt. The Enemy. Houghton, 1951. Story of
the tedium and detail of life aboard a warship during
wartime.

Wouk, Herman. The Caine Mutiny. Doubleday, 1951. Life
aboard a minesweeper in the Pacific under a tyrannical
skipper.

The Tense Years

In the years following World War II a new phase of A-
merican history came into existence. Domestic and international crises erupted at the same time our complacency
and standard of living rose to new heights. On the domestic scene the major force stimulating fiction of the period
was the turmoil of the beginning of the fight for equal rights
for the Negro. The voice of the conservative was heard
again in the land, and is represented in fiction by novels
based on the effects of the Congressional investigations and
the fear aroused by the search for Communists in our midst.
This was just one aspect of our involvement in the Cold War,
which has been used by novelists in a variety of settings;
the interaction of U. S. servicemen and native populations
in occupied countries all over the world; the Berlin Airlift;
the Korean War; adventures behind the Iron Curtain; tales
of spying and intrigue, and the operation of our diplomatic
service in the tense spots around the world. Other novels
set in this period deal with the character of the U. S. Senate, with history of Alaska and Hawaii leading up to statehood, and the development of the United Nations.

Albrand, Martha. Nightmare in Copenhagen. Random, 1954.
    An American scientist attempts to thwart the Russians
    from getting a secret explosive recovered from a Ger-
    man submarine sunk off Denmark in World War II.

Anders, Curtis. The Price of Courage. Sagamore Press,
    1957. Realistic battle scenes as experienced by an

231

infantry company in the Korean War.

Anderson, Thomas. Your Own Beloved Sons. Random,
1956. Authentic setting and military detail revolving
around a dangerous mission by six volunteers in the
Korean War.

Ayer, Frederick. Where No Flags Fly. Regnery, 1960.
Story of a Hungarian-born American scientist who de-
fects behind the Iron Curtain as a spy for the U. S.
Secret Service.

Bartholomew, Cecilia. The Risk. Doubleday, 1958. Story
of the tragic effect on the family of a man who is
declared a security risk because of his friendship with
a known subversive. Recreates the uncertainties and
suspicions of the McCarthy era in the early 1950's.

Beaumont, Charles. The Intruder. Putnam, 1959. Story
of events in a Southern city when a few courageous
citizens react to the trouble stirred up by an outside
rabble rouser who came in to form a pro-segregation
organization.

Boles, Paul Darcy. Deadline. Macmillan, 1957. Story of
a Southern newspaperman's decision to take a stand
against segregation, and of the effects of his decision.

Bonner, Paul Hyde. Hotel Talleyrand. Scribner, 1953.
Story of American diplomatic personnel in Paris in
1950; background is the American effort to check the
growth of Communism in Europe.

---    SPQR. Scribner, 1952. Sophisticated romance centering around a first secretary of the American Embas-
sy in Rome, involving a spy hunt.

Boyle, Kay.  Generation Without Farewell.  Knopf, 1959.
    Story of the relationship between victor and vanquished,
    set in the American occupation zone of Germany in
    1948.

Brooks, Gwendolyn.  Maud Martha.  Harper, 1953.  Story
    of a Negro girl growing up from childhood to mother-
    hood facing discrimination on the South Side in Chicago
    during the 1940's.

Brown, Frank London.  Trumbull Park.  Regnery, 1959.
    Fictional account of the race riots in Trumbull Park,
    a Chicago housing development, in the 1950's.

Buckley, David.  Pride of Innocence.  Holt, 1957.  Story of
    the moral and intellectural disillusionment of a young
    American soldier on occupation duty in Germany after
    World War II.

Burgess, Jackson.  The Atrocity.  Putnam, 1961.  Story of
    a brutal incident and its effect on one U. S. soldier
    in an ordnance company stationed in Italy at the end
    of World War II.

Chatterton, Ruth.  The Betrayers.  Houghton, 1953.  Story
    of the investigation by a Congressional committee of
    a young scientist suspected of subversive activity.

Chevalier, Haakon Maurice.  The Man Who Would be God.
    Putnam, 1959.  An FBI agent is won over to the
    Communist Party by the scientist he is investigating;
    the scientist, cleared for atomic bomb research,
    changes his convictions.

Daniels, Lucy.  Caleb, My Son.  Lippincott, 1956.  Tragic
    story of the effect of segregation upon a family of

Southern Negroes.

Davis, Christopher. First Family. Coward, 1961. Story
of the effects on a white suburban community when a
Negro family moves into the neighborhood.

Drury, Allen. Advise and Consent. Doubleday, 1959. Picture of the workings of the U. S. Senate; story of political and personal conflicts set in motion as the Senate
debates confirmation of the President's nomination for
Secretary of State; issue is the nominee's association
with a student Communist group.

Ehle, John. Move Over, Mountain. Morrow, 1957. Novel
of Negro life in North Carolina complicated by family
rivalries and dreams of "up north."

Flood, Charles Bracelen. A Distant Drum. Houghton,
1957. Story of a young man, graduate of Harvard '51,
writing a first novel and growing to maturity; enlists
in the Army at the time of the Korean War and goes
through basic training before discharge because of a
congenital defect.

Frank, Pat. Hold Back the Night. Lippincott, 1952. Story
of a U. S. Marine unit in Korea covering the retreat
from the Changjin Reservoir to Hungnam on the coast.

Frankel, Ernest. Band of Brothers. Macmillan, 1958.
A story of the Marine retreat from the Yalu River to
Hungnam when the Chinese entered the war in Korea.

---    Tongue of Fire. Dial, 1960. Story of a crusading
Congressman who achieves quick fame through his
Congressional committee investigating supposed Com-
munists; patterned on the career of Senator Joseph Mc

Carthy.

Gallico, Paul. Trial by Terror. Knopf, 1952. Story of
an American newspaperman captured behind the Iron
Curtain and tried as a spy.

Gann, Ernest. Soldier of Fortune. Sloane, 1954. Picture
of Communist China as seen by two Americans search-
ing for the photographer-husband of one of them.

Garrett, George. Which Ones Are the Enemy. Little,
1961. Set in Trieste after World War II, this is a
love story told against a background of U. S. occupation forces and the underground of soldier-gangsters
and black market operators.

Geer, Andrew Clare. Reckless, Pride of the Marines.
Dutton, 1955. Story of a mule mascot of the Fifth U.
S. Marine Regiment who became famous as an ammu-
nition carrier and morale builder in the Korean War.

Gilman, Peter. Diamond Head. Coward, 1960. Recreates
the historical background and the struggle for Hawaiian
statehood from the viewpoint of a present-day family.

Gordon, Arthur. Reprisal. Simon and Schuster, 1950.
Story of race violence in a Georgia town when a young
Negro whose wife had been murdered takes things into
his own hands.

Greene, Harris. The 'Mozart' Leaves at Nine. Doubleday,
1960. A U. S. Army security service chief in Amer-
ican-occupied Austria is busy keeping track of surviv-
ing Nazis and Russian agents in the year after the end
of World War II; story of the effect of the U. S. decision to return a Russian defector.

Gregor, Manfred. Town Without Pity. Random, 1961.
Story of German-American relations in a small German town still occupied by American troops in the late 1950's.

Groninger, William. Run From the Mountain. Rinehart, 1959. Story of the army experiences of a young American soldier in occupied Japan from 1946 to 1949.

Gurney, Hal. Fifth Daughter. Doubleday, 1957. Story of the interactions of the Okinawans and Americans during the occupation following World War II.

Gwaltney, Francis Irby. The Number of Our Days. Random, 1959. A World War II veteran leads a revolt against radical segregationists in his home town in Arkansas following the Supreme Court decision in 1954.

Habe, Hans. Off Limits. Fell, 1957. Story of the relations between Americans and Germans in the U. S. occupied zone of West Berlin, 1945-51.

Hersey, John. A Bell for Adano. Knopf, 1944. Story of the efforts of an understanding American occupation administrator to rebuild a devastated Italian village according to his own democratic ideals.

Hoffman, William. A Place for My Head. Doubleday, 1960. A small town Virginia lawyer successfully defends a Negro's insurance claim but finds the Negro hoped to lose as a propaganda weapon in his race agitation; presents the case of the whites who care for the Negro welfare but want to keep the status quo.

Kern, Alfred. The Width of Waters. Houghton, 1959. Story of the preparations for a sesquicentenial celebra-

tion in a Pennsylvania town, and of the effect of news
that one hometown boy had been killed and another had
become a turncoat in the Korean War.

Kiker, Douglas.  The Southerner.  Rinehart, 1957.  Story of
a school segregation case in a fictional Southern city.

Jackson, Felix.  So Help Me God.  Viking, 1955.  Story of
a young lawyer who sends an anoymous letter to a
Congressional committee accusing himself of being a
Communist in an effort to expose the dangers of con-
demning a man as subversive on the basis of hearsay
evidence; an indictment of the fear and suspicion a-
roused by the McCarthy investigations.

Lorraine, John.  Men of Career.  Crown, 1960.  Story of
the U. S. State Department diplomatic corps in Vienna
in 1953; theme is how the members of the Foreign
Service reacted to the McCarthy loyalty investigations.

McGivern, William.  P. Odds Against Tomorrow.  Dodd,
1957.  Story of two bank robbers, one white, one
Negro, and of their friendship growing out of enmity
during their flight and refuge in an isolated farmhouse.

McGovern, James.  The Berlin Couriers.  Abelard, 1960.
Story of a U. S. intelligence agent in Berlin during the
East German uprising of 1953, sent to interview a de-
fecting scientist; captured by the Russians, he escapes with important documents.

McIlwain, William.  The Glass Rooster.  Doubleday, 1960.
Story of violence following the false accusation that a
young Negro had raped a white woman; set around a
survey of white and Negro recreational facilities in a
Southern town.

MacInnes, Helen. I and My True Love. Harcourt, 1953.
A Washington hostess and a Communist Czech official
are caught between Communist spies and the hysterical
fear of Communists in government.

Maddux, Rachel. Abel's Daughter. Harper, 1960. Story
of a Northern couple who move to a small Southern
town during World War II and come to understand the
practical aspects of the color question in the South
through their friendship with the leader of the Negro
community.

Mankiewicz, Don. Trial. Harper, 1955. Story of the trial
of a young Mexican in a West coast city; Communists
exploit the possibilities of racial prejudice.

Marquand, J. P. Stopover: Tokyo. Little, 1957. American intelligence agents attempt to break up a Communist plot to stage anti-American riots in Japan.

Marshall, Paule. Brown Girl, Brownstones. Random, 1959.
Story of a Negro girl coming to grips with herself and
with life and its prejudices in Brooklyn.

Michener, James. Bridges at Toko-ri. Random, 1953.
Story of a U. S. Navy aircraft carrier task force assigned the mission of bombing enemy supply lines in
the Korean War.

Miller, Waren. The Sleep of Reason. Little, 1960. A
satire on politics in Washington during the McCarthy
era; story of a young man hired to ferret out subversion
for a Senate investigating committee.

Moll, Elick. Seidman and Son. Putnam, 1958. Picture of
the New York dress industry following the Korean War.

Morris, Edita. The Flowers of Hiroshima. Viking, 1959.
An American realizes the horror of the atomic bomb
when he discovers that the Japanese family with whom
he is lodging lost their wife and mother in the 1945
bombing and that the father is dying of radiation sick-
ness.

Pollini, Francis. Night. Houghton, 1961. Life of American prisoners captured by the Chinese during the Korean War; centers around the efforts at brainwashing,
and the conflict and violence between "reactionaries"
and "progressives."

Polonsky, Abraham. A Season of Fear. Cameron, 1956.
Story of the conflicts arising out of the signing of a
loyalty oath by a civil engineer. Convincing picture of
the fear and suspicion made possible by the climate of
opinion in the early 1950's at the time of the McCarthy investigations.

Press, Sylvia. Care of Devils. Beacon, 1958. Story of
the efforts of a woman agent in Washington to clear
her name from the accusations made against her in a
security investigation.

Rogers, Lettie Hamlett. Birthright. Simon and Schuster,
1957. Story of the reactions when a teacher in a
small Southern town praises the Supreme Court decision of 1954.

Romulo, Carlos P. The United. Crown, 1951. Picture of
international diplomacy at work in the United Nations;
story of an alternate U. S. delegate standing up for
his principles against the arguments of a newspaper
columnist and a Boston Brahmin.

Roripaugh, Robert A. A Fever for Living. Morrow, 1961.
Tragic love story set in U. S. occupied Japan, giving
details of life in an army camp.

Salter, James. The Arm of Flesh. Harper, 1961. Vivid
picture of life of the members of a fighter squadron
in an American air base in occupied Germany after
World War II.

Shaw, Irwin. The Troubled Air. Random, 1951. Story of
the disastrous results when a radio program director
is ordered to fire five actors suspected of being Communists.

Scott, Robert L. Look of the Eagle. Dodd, 1955. Story
of jet warfare in the Korean War, and of a scheme to
fly a Russian jet out of North Korea.

Sheldon, Walter. Tour of Duty. Lippincott, 1959. Story of
Japanese-American relations in occupied Japan after
World War II; set on a U. S. Air Force base near a
small Japanese village.

Sinclair, Jo. The Changelings. McGraw, 1955. Story of
a Jewish community in a Midwestern city being press-
ed by a growing Negro population; teen-agers lead their
parents toward tolerance and understanding in the face
of threatening race riots.

Sinclair, Upton. Return of Lanny Budd. Viking, 1953.
Events since the end of World War II bring back Lanny
Budd in this story of the growth of the Russian menace;
takes him to the troubled spots of Europe, from 1946
to 1949. Sequel to "O Shepherd Speak." (World War II).

Singer, Howard. Wake Me When It's Over. Putnam, 1959.

Humorous story of an Air Force radar man who builds
an island resort hotel on his off-duty hours for servicemen on leave from the Korean War.

Slaughter, Frank. Sword and Scalpel. Doubleday, 1957.
Story of an American army officer in the Korean War;
experiences in battle, as a prisoner of the Chinese,
and on trial for collaborating with the Communists.

Smith, William Dale. A Multitude of Men. Simon and Schuster, 1960. Conflict between a company union and
outside labor organizers in a West Virginia steel mill
in the period after the Korean War.

Sneider, Vern. A Pail of Oysters. Putnam, 1953. Story
of an American newspaperman on Formosa, determined
to find the facts behind official camouflage

--- The Teahouse of the August Moon. Putnam, 1951.
Humorous story of an American occupation team and
its efforts to "rehabilitate" and democratize Okinawa
after the war.

Spencer, Elizabeth. The Voice at the Back Door. McGraw,
1956. Story of life in a small Mississippi community,
showing the changing pattern in race relations.

Ullman, James Ramsey. Windom's Way. Lippincott, 1952.
An American doctor in a hospital near a rubber plantation in Southeastern Asia sympathizes with the natives in a strike over their need for more rice land;
strong-arm official action drives some of the people
into the Communist camp.

Voorhees, Melvin. Show Me a Hero. Simon and Schuster,
1954. Story of the Korean War and of the moral di-

lemma of three men, a general, a newspaper reporter, and a private.

Wallis, Arthur and Charles Blair. Thunder Above. Holt, 1956. Story of adventure behind the Iron Curtain when an American plane participating in the Berlin Airlift of 1948-49 is shot down.

Weeks, William Rawle. Knock and Wait Awhile. Houghton, 1957. Story of American counterespionage in postwar Europe, involving an American girl reporter's efforts to hide behind the Iron Curtain.

Wheeler, Keith. Peaceable Lane. Simon and Schuster, 1960. Story of prejudice in a suburban community near New York when neighbors unite in an effort to block the sale of a house to a Negro family.

--- Small World. Dutton, 1958. Story revolving around world affairs from World War II through the Korean War to the Cold War and Communist East Germany as they effect two American newspaper foreign correspondents.

Wright, Richard. The Long Dream. Doubleday, 1958. Story of a Negro boyhood in a Mississippi town; the father became powerful in the Negro community by working with corrupt officials, and in the end the son escapes by flight to France.

--- The Outsider. Harper, 1953. Story of a Negro's search for an ethical identity in Chicago.

Young, Jefferson. A Good Man. Bobbs, 1953. Story of the trouble aroused when a Mississippi Negro tenant farmer planned to paint his house white.

# Chronicles

Adelson, Ann. The Little Conquerors. Random, 1960.
Story of an Italian-American family settling and growing up in a New England town dominated by Irish politicians; time is 1930's to the 1950's.

Aldrich, Bess Streeter. Miss Bishop. Appleton, 1933.
Story of an English teacher in a Midwestern college
facing life from the 1880's to the 1930's.

Appel, Benjamin. A Big Man, a Fast Man. Morrow, 1961.
Story of a labor leader's interviews with a public relations man hired to project a better public image of
him; ranges from the drives to organize labor in the
1930's to the era of the big unions in the 1950's.

Auchincloss, Louis. House of Five Talents. Houghton,
1960. Family chronicle of the rich in Newport and
New York from 1873 to 1948; pictures mansions on
Fifth Avenue, garden parties, the opera, and architecture.

Bacon, Josephine. Root and the Flower. Appleton, 1936.
Development of the position of women in American life
from 1860 to the 1930's.

Blassingame, Wyatt. Live from the Devil. Doubleday,
1959. Story of the Florida cattle country and the development of the modern cattle industry from 1900 to
the 1950's.

Boles, Paul Darcy. Glenport, Illinois. Macmillan, 1956.

Portrays average community life in a small town near
Chicago from 1929 to 1944; the son of an Irish baker
grows up to be a successful band leader until his
death in World War II.

Bourjaily, Vance. The Violated. Dial, 1958. Follows the
lives of four Americans from the prosperous 20's,
through the Depression and World War II, to the prosperous 50's.

Boyd, James. Roll River. Scribner, 1935. Story of four
generations of a Pennsylvania river town family.

Brace, Gerald Warner. The Garretson Chronicle. Norton,
1947. Story of three generations of a New England
family in a village not far from Boston.

Brandon, Evan. Green Pond. Vanguard, 1955. Story of
the medical profession, set in the Carolina red lands
from the Civil War to the present.

Bromfield, Louis. The Farm. Harper, 1933. Ohio farm
and small town life from 1815 to 1915; depicts the
changing manners and patterns of rural social life and
the development of a small Midwestern industrial town.

Burlingame, Roger. Three Bags Full. Harcourt, 1936.
Panorama of life in the Mohawk Valley of New York
from the days of the Holland Land Company to the
present; picture of the change from the log cabins of
pioneer days to mansion and town house as communities
developed.

Carroll, Gladys Hasty. Dunnybrook. Macmillan, 1943.
Fictional biography of the author's family from Revolutionary days. Setting is a Maine village.

--- Sing Out the Glory. Little, 1957. Panorama of U-
nited States history from the turn of the century as it
effects an isolated community in Maine.

Cheever, John. The Wapshopt Chronicle. Harper, 1957.
Picture of family life in an old New England town from
the turn of the century to the present.

Clad, Noel. Love and Money. Random, 1959. Chronicle
of the social and economic history of the United States
from 1917 to 1948; includes anti-German feeling during World War I, the growing movie industry, the jazz
age, the Florida boom, the Depression, the rise of
Hitler, World War II, housing boom following the war,
and the Congressional investigations of the McCarthy
era.

Clune, Henry. By His Own Hand. Macmillan, 1952. Story
of a small segment of American society from 1906
through the Twenties and the post-Depression years of
the Thirties.

Delmar, Viña. The Big Family. Harcourt, 1961. Story of
the Slidell family and of the social and political events
of the country from the Revolution through the 1870's.
Centers around John Slidell, Southern political leader
and Confederate representative to France during the
Civil War.

Downes, Anne Miller. The Eagle's Song. Lippincott, 1949.
Story of a strong-willed family clan and a growing community in the Mohawk River valley of New York from
the Revolution to World War I.

Duncan, Thomas William. Big River, Big Man. Lippincott,
1959. Story of a Wisconsin logger through his rise as

empire builder; life on the Mississippi River, New
Mexico, New England, and the South during the Civil
War are some of the areas touched by the many char-
acters.

Ferber, Edna. American Beauty. Doubleday, 1931. Chronicle of the build-up, the gradual disintegration, and the
rejuvenation of a large estate in Connecticut from 1700
to 1930.

--- Come and Get It. Doubleday, 1935. Story of the rise
and fall of the lumber industry in Wisconsin and Michigan from 1850 to the 1930's.

--- Giant. Doubleday, 1952. Sweeping story of land and
oil rich Texans; 1920's to the present.

--- Ice Palace. Doubleday, 1958. Tale of Alaska from
pioneering days to the movement for statehood.

Fields, Jonathan. The Memoirs of Dunstan Barr. Coward,
1959. Picture of the changing patterns of farm and
small town life and the growth of little business in
Illinois from 1890 to the crash of 1929.

Goddard, Gloria. These Lords' Descendants. Stokes, 1930.
Story of changing American life from Colonial times
to World War I through the fortunes of the descendants
of an English migrant to Colonial America.

Hergesheimer, Joseph. The Limestone Tree. Knopf, 1931.
Chronicle of Kentucky family life from the time of
Daniel Boone through the Civil War to the 1890's.

Holt, Isabella. Golden Moment. Random, 1959. Story of
a woman's marriages set against a background of A-
merican political life from the 1920's through the

Roosevelt era and World War II to the Congressional
loyalty investigations in the 1950's.

Hummel, George Frederick.  Joshua Moore, American.
Doubleday, 1943.  Episodes in American history from
colonization, the American Revolution, settling in Ohio,
anti-slavery riots in Kansas, and expansion in California.

Jenks, Almet.  The Second Chance.  Lippincott, 1950. Story
of a man who missed fighting in World War I; re-
covered from near disaster during the Depression after
entering the financial life of Wall Street in the 1920's;
and is killed in action in World War II.

Keyes, Frances Parkinson.  Crescent Carnival.  Messner,
1942.  New Orleans during fifty years from 1890's to
1940's; details of the carnival season, Louisiana lottery,
fireman's parade, architecture, and social and political
life.

--- The River Road.  Messner, 1945.  Picture of political,
financial, and social conditions in the bayou country of
Louisiana from World War I through World War II.

--- Steamboat Gothic.  Messner, 1952.  Family chronicle
which reflects fluctuations in the economic life and
describes the customs and manners of plantation and
river life on the lower Mississippi River from 1870
to 1930.

Lockridge, Ross.  Raintree County.  Houghton, 1948. Story
of Raintree County, Indiana from 1844 to 1892, showing historical events as the hero, who kept coming
back to his home county, saw them.

Longman, M. B. (pseud.) The Power of Black. Globus,
1961. Epic story of three generations of a Southern
family who lose everything in the Civil War, begin
over in the Texas oil fields, and follow the fluctuations of the oil industry through the post-World War I
era.

Marquand, J. P. Haven's End. Little, 1933. Chronicle
of a New England town through three generations of a
family whose prosperity was based on slave running.

--- The Late George Apley. Little, 1937. Life story of
a member of a Beacon Hill family. Pictures the life
and customs of aristocratic Boston in the period from
the 1880's to 1933.

--- Sincerely, Willis Wayde. Little, 1949. Story of the
rise of a successful industrialist, picturing the impact
of changes in the American economic scene from the
turn of the century to the 1940's.

Martin, Peter. The Building. Little, 1960. Story of the
immigration of a Jewish family from Russia to upstate
New York in the early 1900's, and of their business
and family life to the 1930's.

Michener, James. Hawaii. Random, 1959. An epic history of the Hawaiian Islands from ancient times to the
successful struggle for statehood.

Mills, Charles. The Alexandrians. Putnam, 1952. Panorama of the changing patterns of life in a small Georgia town from its first settlement in 1839 until the day
of its centennial celebration.

Moody, Minnie Hite. Long Meadow. Macmillan, 1941.

Chronicle of the Hite family from 1705 to the 1860's
when two of the cousins died in the Civil War, one
fighting for the South, the other for the Union.

Moore, Ruth. Speak to the Winds. Morrow, 1956. Three
generations of the families who, in 1855, developed a
town on an island off the Maine coast to exploit the
granite found there.

Morris, Hilda. The Long View. Putnam, 1937. A three-
generation family chronicle showing the changing patterns of life from the Civil War through the Depression; New Jersey, rural New York, Indiana, Chicago,
and Europe.

Norris, Frank. Tower in the West. Harper, 1957. Picture of American social and economic life from the
Twenties to World War II through the life history of
a revolutionary skyscraper hotel in St. Louis; Prohibition, the crash of 1929, the Depression, recovery,
and prosperity through World War II.

O'Hara, John. From the Terrace. Random, 1958. Study
of the life of a member of the wealthy class from boyhood through service in World War I, career in the
early aviation industry and in Wall Street financial
circles, and government service in World War II.

Powell, Richard. The Philadelphian. Scribner, 1956.
Story of social life and customs seen through four generations of a Philadelphia family from 1857 to the
present.

Rawlings, Marjorie Kinnan. The Sojourner. Scribner,
1953. Life on a farm in upstate New York from 1880
to World War II.

Robinson, Henry Morton. Water of Life. Simon and Schuster, 1960. American social and political events from the post-Civil War period through Prohibition in the background of this history of the whiskey making industry.

Rooney, Frank. The Courts of Memory. Vanguard, 1954. Story of modern family life from 1930's to the present; set in Los Angeles and New York.

Sandburg, Carl. Remembrance Rock. Harcourt, 1948. Panorama of American history from the days of the Pilgrims to the end of World War II.

Seton, Anya. The Hearth and Eagle. Houghton, 1948. Story of Marblehead, Massachusetts from its earliest settlement to the present.

Siebel, Julia. The Narrow Covering. Harcourt, 1956. Life in a small town in Kansas from before World War I to the years following Pearl Harbor.

Stegner, Wallace. The Big Rock Candy Mountain. Duell, 1943. Life in the Far West and in Saskatchewan Province of Canada from 1906 to 1942.

Stevens, Louis. Days of Promise. Prentice, 1948. Panorama of American society from the Civil War to the 1940's told through the chronicle of a Kansas newspaper family.

Tute, Warren. Leviathan. Little, 1959. A story of the steamship industry; the building and operating of a great liner from its launching in the 1930's to its sinking in service as a troop carrier during World War II.

Walker, Mildred. Curlew's Cry. Harcourt, 1955. Picture of ranch life in Montana from 1905 to the 1940's.

Watson, Virginia. Manhattan Acres. Dutton, 1934. Picture of the growth of New York City; chronicle of a
Dutch family from the 1630's to 1933.

Wescott, Glenway. The Grandmothers. Harper, 1927.
Chronicle of a Wisconsin family, one of those who
helped settle the frontier, from the 1840's through the
Civil War to the turn of the century.

White, William Allen. A Certain Rich Man. Macmillan,
1909. Story of a millionaire industralist and the
growth of his Kansas town from the Civil War to the
turn of the century.

Wight, Frederick. Chronicle of Aaron Kane. Farrar, 1936.
Story of the long life of a Scotch-Irish Cape Cod sailor
from 1838 through the post-Civil War years.

Wilder, Robert. The Sun Is My Shadow. Putnam, 1960.
Story of a woman's career in newspaper work; economic and political events from the late 1920's
through the Depression, the Roosevelt era, the rise of
Hitler, and World War II.

Williams, Ben Ames. The Strange Woman. Houghton,
1941. Story of a wicked but beautiful woman, extend-
ing in time from the War of 1812 through the Civil
War with Maine as its scene.

Wilson, Mitchell. Live with Lightning. Little, 1949. Story
of the career of a young physicist, from his years as
laboratory assistant during the Depression of the thirties, to industrial scientist, to atomic research worker

during World War II and after.

The Literature of Historical Fiction

Few comprehensive studies have been made of historical fiction. The standard bibliographies of Baker and Nield have had new editions issued through the years and are still in use. Hannah Logasa's "Historical Fiction" has gone through seven editions, and "America in Fiction" by Coan and Lillard was issued in a fourth edition in 1956.

Historical fiction has been especially neglected in recent years in the realm of critical studies. As a literary form it was dealt with by Brander Matthews in "The Historical Novel and Other Essays," by Herbert Butterfield in "The Historical Novel," by Ernest E. Leisy in his introduction to "The American Historical Novel," and in a number of illuminating essays, written chiefly by historical novelists and critics in such magazines as "The Saturday Review," "The Atlantic Monthly," and "The New Republic".

Perhaps the single outstanding survey and critical study of American historical fiction is Ernest E. Leisy's "The American Historical Novel." This book serves a double purpose: as a guide to fiction dealing with different periods of American history, and as a critical evaluation of the novels treated within each historical period. Each title discussed in the body of the work is analyzed for content and theme, evaluated from the standpoint of literary and/or historical merit, and related to other novels dealing with the same subject. An introduction, "History Vivified," and the Conclusion attempt to define historical fiction and discuss the genre as

a whole. An appendix lists and briefly annotates additional
titles which are not discussed in the text.

The work of a few recognized historical novelists is
discussed in "The Modern Novel in America, 1900-1950" by
Frederick J. Hoffman, a survey and critical study of American fiction of the first half of this century. Hoffman dis-
cusses the work of Willa Cather, Ellen Glasgow, Edith
Wharton, and Elizabeth Maddox Roberts, among others.
Edward Wagenknecht, in "Cavalcade of the American Novel,"
devotes a section of his chapter on the novelist of the 1930's
to what he calls "Return to History." Margaret Mitchell,
Hervey Allen, Kenneth Roberts, Esther Forbes, Howard
Fast, August Derleth, and Conrad Richter receive lengthy
treatment, while others are briefly mentioned in this section.
The work of Mary Johnston, Willa Cather, Frank Norris,
Edith Wharton, Ellen Glasgow, Elsie Singmaster, Joseph
Hergesheimer, Hemingway, and Dos Passos are analyzed in
earlier chapters. Any student of historical fiction and its
writers will find Wagenknecht's book of great value.

Historical fiction has received perhaps its broadest
treatment in magazines. The relationships of historical
novelist to the historian is the subject of Arthur S. Tourtellot in "History and the Historical Novelist" in "Saturday Review of Literature" (August 20, 1940). Tourtellot's thesis
is that while the historian is free to look at a historical
period with a critical eye, to pass judgements on the past
in the light of what happened afterwards, the historical
novelist has no such freedom; he can expose no more know-
ledge of a historical event and of its consequences than
what his characters could know. The historical novelist
must place himself fully into the past and experience the

action as he writes about it.

Tourtellot cites the Erie Canal novels of Walter D. Edmonds as an example of the historical novelist's ability to deal extensively with a limited area, while the historian can do no more than generalize. Edmonds' novels are the subject of a critical essay by Robert M. Gay, "The Historical Novel: Walter D. Edmonds," in "The Atlantic Monthly" (May, 1946). Gay attributes Edmonds' success to his ability to convey the spiritual and mental atmosphere of the time and place in which his novels were set, an atmosphere unique to each era.

John Farrar, in "Novelists and/or Historians" in "Saturday Review of Literature" (February 17, 1945), offers a word of advice to the new writer who may be tempted to write historical novels on the mistaken impression that it is easier to write a successful novel with a historical background. The new writer, he advises, would be wise to write history as non-fiction, but, if he must write historical novels, he should be sure that he is novelist first, and historical novelist afterward, a thought seconded by Esther Forbes in her essay, "Historical Novels" in "Saturday Review of Literature" (April 23, 1949). Robert Gay expressed the same thought when he said, "Whatever makes a novel good makes a historical novel good; and that is a story that moves and characters that live."

There are dissenting voices, as, indeed there are historical novels which do not measure up to the requirements of a good novel. The literary editor of "Newsweek Magazine" (October 30, 1950), in a review appropriately entitled "Anything Goes," indicates his conception of the historical novel as a "specialized department of current fiction, with its own conventions and formalities." Edward Fitzgerald,

in "Fact, Fiction, or Fantasy," in "The Saturday Review"
(January 17, 1953), comments on the fact that the popularity
of historical fiction is based on escapism and sex appeal.
He calls this the sex phantasy of the American housewife.
Siegfried Mandel, in "You Are There" in "The Saturday Review" (August 8, 1953), expresses a similar idea when he
implies that interest in historical fiction is based on the
extra appeal of justifiable escapism.  He says, "The liberal
sprinkling of history gives the reader a feeling of informative gain, above and beyond the usual pleasure of reading
for reading's sake."  This is not so much a valid comment
on the historical novel as it is an indication of the too usual
indentification of the sex and swordplay period piece as the
only form of historical fiction.

In "The Insides of a Novel" in "The Atlantic Monthly"
(February, 1946), Bruce Lancaster tells of some of the details which must be hunted down and assimilated before the
writer begins to write his historical novel, and Ben Ames
Williams, in "Fiction's Fourth Dimension" in "Saturday
Review of Literature" (October 16, 1948), gives his personal
aims and methods as an historical novelist.

A bird's eye view of post-World War II American fiction is given by Malcolm Cowley in "American Fiction Since
the War" in "The New Republic" (December 28, 1953). The
greater part of his essay is concerned with World War II
novels.  In essence, Cowley feels that, with a few exceptions, novels dealing with the war are so much alike that
dialogue and episodes could be transferred from one to the
other with little change.  Another incisive discussion of
World War II novels may be found in "If You Write About
The War," a critical essay by Irwin Shaw in "Saturday

Review of Literature" (February 17, 1945).

An able defense of writers of contemporary historical fiction is presented by John Hersey, along with a formulation of their aims and motivations, in "The Novel of Contemporary History" in "The Atlantic Monthly" (November, 1949). Hersey states that the "genre of the contemporary historical novel is indistinguishable from that of the historical novel in general. Indeed the superior novel of contemporary events will in time come to be regarded as a historical novel."

The following bibliography, while not complete, may serve as a stepping stone and guide to the fascinating study of America's past in fiction.

### Books

Baker, Ernest A. History in Fiction; a Guide to the Best Historical Romances, Sagas, Novels, and Tales. 2 vols. London: George Routledge & Sons, n.d.

Boynton, Percy H. America in Contemporary Fiction. Chicago: The University of Chicago Press, 1940,

--- The Rediscovery of the American Frontier. Chicago: The University of Chicago Press, 1931.

Butterfield, Herbert. The Historical Novel: an Essay. Cambridge: The Cambridge University Press, 1924.

Coan, Otis and Lillard, Richard G. America in Fiction: an Annotated List of Novels That Interpret Aspects of Life in the United States. 4th ed. Stanford: The Stanford University Press, 1956.

Haines, Helen E. What's in a Novel. New York: The Columbia University Press, 1942.

Hart, James D. The Popular Book, a History of America's Literary Taste. New York: Oxford University Press, 1950.

Hoffman, Frederick J.  The Modern Novel in America,
    1900-1950.  Chicago:  The Henry Regnery Co., 1951.

--- The Twenties:  American Writing in the Postwar Dec-
    ade.  New York:  Viking Press, 1955.

Leisy, Ernest E.  The American Historical Novel.  Norman:
    The University of Oklahoma Press, 1950.

Lively, Robert A.  Fiction Fights the Civil War.  Raleigh:
    The University of North Carolina Press, 1957.

Logasa, Hannah.  Historical Fiction: Guide for Junior and
    Senior High Schools, and Colleges, also for General
    Reader.  7th Revised and Enlarged Edition.  Phila-
    delphia:  McKinley Publishing Co., 1960.

Matthews, Brander.  Historical Novel and Other Essays.
    New York:  Scribner, 1901.

Nield, Jonathan.  A Guide to the Best Historical Novels and
    Tales.  5th ed.  New York:  The Macmillan Co., 1929.

Thiessen, N. J.  Annotated Bibliography of American His-
    torical Fiction.  Emporia:  Kansas State Teachers
    College, 1938.

Van Doren, Carl.  The American Novel, 1789-1939.  New
    York:  The Macmillan Co., 1940.

Wagenknecht, Edward.  Cavalcade of the American Novel
    From the Birth of the Nation to the Middle of the
    Twentieth Century.  New York:  Henry Holt & Co.,
    1952.

## Articles

Aaron, Daniel.  Epic is Yet to be Written, American Herit-
    age, IX, October, 1958, 112.

Anything Goes, Newsweek Magazine, XXXVI, October 30,
    1950, 84.

Beale, Howard K.  What Historians Have Said About the
    Causes of the Civil War, in Theory and Practice in
    Historical Study.  A Report of the Committee on His-

toriography.  New York:  Social Science Research
Council, 1946.

Bristow, Gwen.  You-Are-Thereness, Writer, LXXII, October, 1959, 8.

Cowley, Malcolm.     American Novels Since the War, New
Republic, CXXIX, December 28, 1953, 16.

Farrar, John.  Novelists and/or Historians, Saturday Review of Literature, XXVIII, February 17, 1945, 7.

Fitzgerald, Edward J.  Fact, Fiction, or Fantasy, The
Saturday Review, XXXVI, January 17, 1953, 13.

Forbes, Esther.  Historical Novels, Saturday Review of
Literature, XXXII, April 23, 1949, 7.

Gay, Robert M.  The Historical Novel:  Walter D. Edmonds,
The Atlantic Monthly, CLXV, May, 1940, 656.

Harwell, Richard D.  Gone With Miss Ravenel's Courage,
or, Bugles Blow So Red; a Note on the Civil War
Novel, Pacific Northwest Library Association Quarterly
XXV, January, 1961, 110.

Hersey, John.  The Novel of Contemporary History, The
Atlantic Monthly, CLXXXIV, November, 1949, 80.

Lancaster, Bruce.  The Insides of a Novel, The Atlantic
Monthly, CLXXVII, February, 1946, 75.

Mandel, Siegfried.  You Are There!, The Saturday Review,
XXXVI, August 8, 1953, 17.

Research and Imagination, Newsweek Magazine, XXIV, April,
30, 1951, 84.

Shaw, Irwin.  If You Write About the War, Saturday Review
of Literature, XXVIII, February 17, 1945, 5.

Tourtellot, Arthur B.  History and the Historical Novel,
Saturday Review of Literature, XXII, August 20, 1940,
3.

Smith, William James,  War Novel, Commonweal, LXIV,
May 11, 1956, 146.

Stone, Irving.  The Biographical Novel, Writer, LXXV,
    January, 1962, 9.

Waldmeir, Joseph.  Novelists of Two Wars, Nation,
    CLXXXVII, November 1, 1958, 304.

Weales, Gerald.  War and Its Chroniclers, New Republic,
    CXXXVII, October 21, 1957, 18.

Wickson, Ethelwyn.  Workshop in Historical Fiction, On-
    tario Library Review, XLI, November, 1957, 289.

Williams, Ben Ames.  Fiction's Fourth Dimension, Saturday
    Review of Literature, XXXI, October 16, 1948, 8.

Williams, T. Harry.  Review of "Thaddeus Stevens," New
    York Times Book Review, October 30, 1955, 42.

Yerby, Frank.  How and Why I Write the Costume Novel,
    Harper, CCXIX, October, 1959, 145.


### Unpublished Theses

Bertram, Ray Martin.  The Novel of America's Past: A
    Study of Five American Historical Novelists, 1925-
    1950.  Unpublished Doctoral dissertation, School of
    Graduate Studies, the University of Michigan, 1954.

Choate, Julian Ernest, Jr.  The Myth of the American Cow-
    boy: A Study of the Cattleman's Frontier in History
    and Fiction.  Unpublished Master's thesis, Department
    of English, Vanderbilt University, 1954.

Cryder, Robert William.  Some Characteristics of Best-
    Selling Historical Novels: An Analysis of Selected
    Popular Novels, 1930-1950.  Unpublished Master's
    thesis, The Graduate Library School, The University
    of Chicago, 1955.

Duvall, Severn Parker Costin, Jr.  The Legend of the South
    and Southern Historical Fiction, 1820-1861.  Unpub-
    lished Doctoral dissertation, The Graduate School,
    Princeton University, 1955.

Feigenbaum, Lawrence H.  War, As Viewed by the Postwar
    Novelist of World Wars I and II.  Unpublished Doctoral

dissertation, Graduate School of Arts and Sciences, New York University, 1951.

Gast, Marie A. Depression Era as Reflected in the American Novel. Unpublished Master's thesis, School of Library Science, Western Reserve University, 1951.

Graham, Norman. World War II in Fiction: An Annotated, Indexed Bibliography of Adult Novels, Short Story Collections, and Anthologies Published in the United States, 1939-1956. Unpublished Master's thesis, Florida State University, 1958.

Hartin, John Sykes. Southeastern United States in the Novel Through 1950; A Bibliographic Review. Unpublished Doctoral dissertation, School of Graduate Studies, The University of Michigan, 1956.

Loewen, Peter F. The Historical Novel: A Study in the Deviations From the Scott Canon. Unpublished Doctoral dissertation, Department of English, The University of Denver, 1953.

MacKenzie, Carol Alene. Study of Trends in Subject Content of Historical Fiction by American Authors, 1916-1956- Unpublished Master's thesis. Western Reserve University, 1957.

Most, Ralph C. Civil War Fiction, 1890-1920. Unpublished Doctoral dissertation, Department of English, University of Pennsylvania, 1954.

Phipps, Frank T. The Image of War in America, 1891-1917; A Study of a Literary Theme and its Cultural Origins and Analogues. Unpublished Doctoral dissertation, Department of English, Ohio State University, 1954.

Spencer, Marjorie J. Analysis of Ten Illinois Historical Novels for Revelation of Illinois History. Unpublished Master's thesis, Department of Library Science, Texas State College for Women, 1951.

Weber, John S. The American War Novel Dealing With the Revolutionary and Civil Wars. Unpublished Doctoral dissertation, School of Graduate Studies, The University of Wisconsin, 1948.

Index